Ramen Noodles, Rent and Resumes

"*Ramen Noodles, Rent and Resumes* should be given to every college graduate along with their diploma! This is a great read that paints a realistic picture of life after college and offers invaluable tips for how to deal with this time of transition. Kristen Fischer's honest and candid perspective along with the stories from other twenty-somethings make this book relatable to any twenty-something dealing with life in the 'real world.'"

—CHRISTINE HASSLER, AUTHOR OF *TWENTY-SOMETHING, TWENTY-EVERYTHING* AND *THE TWENTY-SOMETHING MANIFESTO*

"Kristen Fischer provides a great guide for all the things you can't learn in college. From the practical to the emotional, this book will help you through the challenges and opportunities of the post-college world."

—LINDSEY POLLAK, AUTHOR OF *GETTING FROM COLLEGE TO CAREER*

"Very few books prepare students for the reality of post-college life, but in *Ramen Noodles, Rent and Resumes*, Kristen Fischer dispels some of the most common myths about making this difficult transition. From finding a job to avoiding the dreaded quarterlife crisis to moving back home with the parents, Fischer packs this practical guide with common sense and key strategies, making it the must-get gift for every grad on your list."

—ELINA FURMAN, AUTHOR OF *BOOMERANG NATION* AND *THE EVERYTHING AFTER COLLEGE BOOK*

"*Ramen Noodles, Rent and Resumes* provides genuine personal experiences and valuable lessons of young adults as they graduated college and began their journey of making crucial choices about their employment, housing and everyday life. This book provides a wealth of expert advice on money management for young adults and students. Not only is this book a great read, but it is a tool that should be given to every student as they enter college as a preparation tool to map out their college education and future."

—DR. TAFFY WAGNER, AUTHOR OF *DEBT DILEMMA*

Ramen Noodles, Rent and Resumes

An After-College Guide to Life

Kristen Fischer

Ramen Noodles, Rent and Resumes: An After-College Guide to Life
By Kristen Fischer

Published by SuperCollege, LLC
3286 Oak Court
Belmont, CA 94002
www.supercollege.com

Credits: Cover: TLC Graphics, www.TLCGraphics.com. Design: Monica Thomas Layout: The Roberts Group, www.editorialservice.com

Trademarks: All brand names, product names and services used in this book are trademarks, registered trademarks or tradenames of their respective holders. SuperCollege is not associated with any college, university, product or vendor.

Disclaimers: The author and publisher have used their best efforts in preparing this book. It is sold with the understanding that the author and publisher are not rendering legal or other professional advice. The author and publisher cannot be held responsible for any loss incurred as a result of specific decisions made by the reader. The author and publisher make no representations or warranties with respect to the accuracy or completeness of the contents of the book and specifically disclaim any implied warranties or merchantability or fitness for a particular purpose. The accuracy and completeness of the information provided herein and the opinions stated herein are not guaranteed or warranted to produce any particular results. The author and publisher specifically disclaim any responsibility for any liability, loss or risk, personal or otherwise, which is incurred as a consequence, directly or indirectly, from the use and application of any of the contents of this book.

ISBN: 1932662251
ISBN13: 9781932662252

Manufactured in the United States of America
10 9 8 7 6 5 4 3 2 1

Cataloging-in-Publication Data
Kristen Fischer

    Ramen Noodles, Rent and Resumes: An After-College Guide to Life
        p. cm.
    ISBN: 1932662251
    ISBN13: 9781932662252
    1. Self-Help   I. Title
    2. Reference   3. Careers

For my mother,
who made my college education possible.

CONTENTS

ACKNOWLEDGEMENTS

A huge thanks to Kelly and Gen Tanabe, who believed in my idea and made it into this book. I am indebted to my entire family, which has provided me with inspiration and support—especially Mommy, Danielle, Mom, and Dad (my agent). My husband is my very best friend and the love of my life, who makes it worth living. And my awesome college buddies have become lifelong friends that I value. Thank you to all of the interviewees in this book who candidly shared part of their lives with me.

God has continued to guide and bless me, and I am forever grateful.

INTRODUCTION

It was May 6, 2000, when I put on that black gown and awkward square cap. My classmates and I were called into line and I sobbed the entire way as we marched into the makeshift graduation arena. The parking lot where our ceremony was held was outlined by the pine trees, which were everywhere at The Richard Stockton College of New Jersey. As we took our seats, I continued to cry. Frying out in the sun on that hot afternoon on black macadam with my family looking on, I was not only distraught—I was also filled with dread.

On that day, in that time, I knew my life was about to change. It would never be quite like it had been during the past four years. I didn't know what it would be like, and I couldn't imagine that anything else could compare to my amazing college experience. In fact, I didn't want to. I was not only happy at college, but I was happy avoiding the "real world." I didn't want my life to change.

Of course, not having to go to class anymore would be a plus—I was never one for schoolwork. But as a student who was really involved in college extracurricular activities, I didn't want to leave the friends I made while being a part of organizations that I had grown to love. To Circle K International, a national service organization, I was a club president and a district governor. To my campus, I was an admissions ambassador and an RA. Heck, I was even the homecoming queen one year. Life at Stockton was perfect for me. I lived far enough from home that I could have my own life, but close enough to drive back to Mom's when I wanted to.

If it could have all stayed that way, I would have let it. I thought life after college would be boring. I did not believe anything really interesting or exciting would ever happen again. College had been *so* wonderful for me that I wasn't looking forward to going to work each day and settling into a life of monotony. Plus, I had no idea why I had never second-guessed my major: environmental studies. I had picked the school based on the program, but I became so involved in campus life from the minute I arrived that I never gave much thought to what that major would mean for my future. But ever since a month before when the school audited my transcripts for graduation, I knew that I didn't want to be an environmental scientist. Sure, I'd eventually get a job and grow up, but I didn't want one that dealt with pollution, water, or dirt. I would have rather lived in my dorm, surrounded by friends and fun activities. Class was just an obligation, a payment, if you will, for living my fabulous collegiate life at that small southern New Jersey school.

I ruminated over hundreds of memories, which all seem to have occurred in the general vicinity of where I sat. I looked to my left, at the field where I spent my first afternoon at Stockton for orientation activities. I remembered the feel of the grass when I kneeled to go through get-to-know-you's with the other freshmen. My mother and sister had just dropped me off at school. While frightened, I knew sitting in that field that I would do well there. Next, I looked past the gym, over to my dorm. In four years of thrills, heartbreaks, bad days and parties, it had always been there to give me a haven away from home. To my right was the parking lot, which served as a landmark I arrived back "home" at school when I pulled in after another trip across the state to visit other Circle K chapters. Finally, past more pine trees in the distance were the academic buildings where I had eagerly taken a myriad of courses and, yes, struggled painstakingly with chemistry and statistics. All the memories flashed before me—good and bad. To me, they were *the* times of my life. What lay ahead was . . . void.

Suddenly, I was called on stage to receive the piece of paper—or the empty frame for it—that actually said I was certifiably ready to graduate. To Stockton, I was the complete graduate. I possessed 128 credits and I was ready to be released out into the world. But I didn't want to go. I received my degree and smiled even though I was crying on the inside. I didn't even want them to mail the diploma to me six weeks later. I would take the empty certificate holder; but I didn't want my degree. Getting that meant I would have to leave everything I loved. Getting that meant I would have to enter the real world, which I felt completely unprepared to do.

Maybe I should go back for my Master's degree, I thought to myself. *Maybe I could stay another year and take some independent studies. Maybe I should run for another office in Circle K so I have to stay in school.* This is what ran through my mind on "May Day" after I received my degree and waited for the ceremony to wrap up. After it did, I was somehow frozen while sunburned. I hugged my friends and looked around as people scattered to squeeze their loved ones and yell out in celebration. It was over. All that was left to do was turn in my key to the Residential Life Office and say goodbye. There was nothing more for me there, as much as I wanted there to be. It was over.

Life has a way of pulling us through times of transition. It's not easy, but somehow we look back and realize we were once in a completely different place. For me, it hit me a few days later that I was in the real world. Even without a job lined up, I was still there. Living in my mother's basement, I was still there. As much as I internally refused to leave college behind, it was inevitable that life had to go on. So I got a job. A few months later, I got an apartment. I went through the motions. And I mourned the loss of my life in college. My degree seemed to stare me down in the face, asking what the heck I was doing when I took a job as a newspaper reporter instead of pursuing a job in the environmental industry, like I was *supposed* to do. Everything seemed to hit me a thousand times harder than I had imagined. What hit me the most was this feeling of impending doom when I envisioned my future. What was next? *Nothing,* I thought to myself, *I've already done it all.*

When I think about my yearning to stay in school and my bleak outlook at the time, I know a lot of it was because I loved my life there and didn't want it to end. But a lot of that resistance was also based on

the fear that I wasn't ready to enter the real world professionally because I never thought it would be enjoyable. I had spent so much time
and effort getting my degree that I didn't know what I was supposed
to do with it. Knowing it was in a field I didn't want to pursue, I felt it
was null and void. All I had been told to do was get a job. Never one
to do something without some sort of meaning, I found it extremely
difficult to simply take a position to earn money. For me, there had
to be something more to life. At the time, I think I relied on college
to miraculously prepare me for that transition. When it didn't, I felt
alone, fearful and bitter.

I'd heard that college prepares you for the real world. But what no
one tells you is that college is just a *platform* to prepare you for the real
world. I realized at the time, and know more so now, that most students were not like me. They were excited to start their lives, eager to
move on—I thought college was my real life and couldn't go forward.
But even the majority of students who are thrilled to start writing the
next chapter of their lives come to the same screeching halt—in one
way or another—as I did. It's inevitable to be overcome by doubt and
fear, and to ask yourself questions like, "What do I want to do with
my life?" and "Is this what I *should* be doing with my life?" I think in
one way or another, even if you were unlike me and eager to graduate,
you'll go through some sort of uncertainty before or after you graduate.
I call it "The After-College."

The After-College is not a quarterlife crisis, though you may experience that during it. The After-College is that time—a few months
up to a few years—after you graduate that you find your place in the
world. It's that period when you're establishing your career and adult
relationships, setting yourself up financially and learning how to live
independently. Most of all, The After-College is an exciting time—not
necessarily a crisis—filled with good experiences that serve as the foundation for who you become as an adult. I think this time can easily
be blown off as a quarterlife crisis, but I have found that too many
students wind up perceiving the years after college as negative if they

think like that. While there are hard times during The After-College, you can thrive during it and learn from it, using it as a growing period that will serve you well during the rest of your life.

I'm a little older and wiser now. I know there is more to life . . . college is just the starting point. I've learned that just because you leave a place you love, it doesn't mean that you cannot cherish the memories or that you cannot go back while still forging into the future. I've learned not to regret giving my all to my college experience, going beyond academics to make an imprint in the world, because it made me a better person. I've learned that I am a richer person for doing so many extraordinary things while I was 18, 19, 20, and 21—that's why it was so painful to leave those experiences behind. I realize that many of you reading this may wonder why I cherished college so much. I didn't; I relished the people I met and the experiences I had during those four years. When it was time to leave, I thought I would lose it all. When it was time to look forward, I kept looking back because I didn't see anything on the horizon. At the time, I knew I had to move ahead, and I did my best to do that by getting a job and getting my own apartment. It wasn't until I found new meaning in my life that I was able to let go. Finally, I am able to look back fondly on my college days, while eagerly facing my future.

This isn't a book about how to let go of college memories—I used my personal story to illustrate how the transition of college will come at you fast and can disorient you. This is a book about what happens *after* "May Day." It's about how we transition into our adult lives. Some of you may struggle to find a solid career, while others may have a hard time moving back with your parents. Regardless of what you struggle with, this book provides interesting, real-life anecdotes from people who have been there and survived. The goal? To make you feel a little more at ease about entering the real world. To help you know what to expect so you can deal with it rationally. After all, the trials you face throughout the rest of your life will come at you quickly just like the end of college does, if not quicker. So The After-College is a period of intense learning and preparation for the rest of your life. (And you thought it ended at graduation? Nope.)

Hopefully by reading this book, potential graduates will learn what to expect when their "May Day" happens. Recent graduates can identify with the situations that the dozens of people I interviewed went through. Those who left college long ago can reminisce about life in their early 20s and see how far they've come since they left college as a wide-eyed graduate. Whether you've clung to your dorm life like me or couldn't wait to bust out of campus, you'll gain perspective about life after college.

I compiled this book because not many people talk about the hardships that can ensue after college. Today's graduates face more options—and financial burdens—than ever before. There are tough decisions to be made when it comes to careers, living situations and relationships. It can be difficult to figure out where you want to go when you realize that your degree wasn't a cure-all and that you don't know what the heck you're doing with your life. The good news is that you're not alone. Whether you're in a quarterlife crisis or not, I believe that reading about the experiences of others will help prepare you for what lies ahead so you can bravely face—and *embrace*—your future as a 20-something. (Oh, and let's not forget enjoying it, because life after college does have its advantages!)

Along the way, I'll share some of my story with you. I'll tell you how I emerged into the real world and learned to accept and thrive in my adult life. *We can all do this by simply experiencing life, including the hard times.* For example, as much as I wanted to hide after I graduated, I didn't. I got out there and took a few jobs until I found what I loved doing. I scraped by on ramen noodles so I could experience living on my own. It wasn't easy. I do believe I went through a quarterlife crisis too. But I'm a better person for it. I've also learned that The After-College isn't a time to suffer through and try to forget about when it's over. If you live it right, it can be better than college.

Here I am, nearly eight years later, and wonderful things have happened to me. I have a career that I love. I have fantastic friends. I have an even more awesome husband. I own a house. Sure, I had to face my innermost demons to get here. But you know what? It's not just the end result . . . everything I experienced and learned along the way was just as thrilling and just as wonderful! Making my way through all of the post-college issues made me who I am—and life is a valuable teacher. I invite you to open your mind to all the possibilities that exist for you as a new graduate. There will be ups and downs as you take your first steps into The After-College, working, living and loving. If you learn to embrace it—and prepare yourself for it too—the ride will be well worth it.

Contrary to my previous beliefs, my life did not end on May 6, 2000. In fact, that's when it really began.

CHAPTER 1
The After-College

"You mean, I'm not doomed for a Quarterlife Crisis?"

When I set out to write this book, I did so to shed light on the myriad of issues that young adults face as they emerge from college. With so many things hitting recent grads—entering the work world, managing finances, finding romance, maintaining friendships, and dealing with parents as an adult, just to name a few—I knew that there was no one answer that could miraculously solve the problems that plague 20-somethings. Rather, this portion of your life—The After-College—is meant for exploration and growth. While every young adult faces a challenge or two that can become a hardship, real-world experience is the greatest teacher. College was just the starting point. It can hit you like a thousand bricks until you feel the impact after you graduate, realize that you're an adult, and say, "Okay, now what?"

When I graduated, I didn't realize that I would get pummeled so hard. Before long, I was thrust into an obscure world where I had to pay my own bills, decipher my career goals and determine what I wanted out of relationships. There was no guide for me until I stumbled upon a book about the "quarterlife crisis." Immediately, I identified with this concept. But I also knew that just because it was a crisis, it didn't mean I should discount the time in my life as "bad." On the reverse, The After-College is thrilling and exciting. Sure, it's a little chaotic, but all transitions are. The big difference is that today's graduates are stepping into a world that *understands* your 20s can be tumultuous. They realize people go through quarterlife crises upon graduation. More people have degrees, and because of that, everyone has more options. Most parents know that you aren't stepping into the same job market they faced, so they can't give you the same advice their parents gave them. The costs of education are so high that graduation means all sorts of financial pressure on new graduates (many of whom have to take low-paying jobs, which makes it hard to get ahead money-wise). Think you'll step out of your cap and gown into a suit and a fancy new pad making $50,000 a year? Dream on. This is not the case for most of today's graduates, and that can be a shocker for many grads. So, what can you do when life after graduation doesn't go as you had planned? Don't fight it—embrace it. This is a messy time in your life. No one has it put all together. They just think that because they have a degree, they should. Wrong again!

Prior to publishing this book, I celebrated—rather, I observed—my 29th birthday. There were two things about 29 that left me spinning. First, my 30s were just around the corner and there are a slew of expectations placed on women in their 30s. Also, it was my last year as a 20-something. While I can tell you that having gone through my 20s I know that all the trials 20-somethings face can be like a living hell, I can also say that if you use them to discover what you want out of life, they will at least prove worth the trouble. While your early 20s especially can be a puzzling time, life in your 20s can also include some of the most carefree, happy memories that you'll have.

I realize that I'm not going through my quarterlife crisis anymore, and that I've moved out of my After-College. I also know that I'm writing to an audience that is thick into The After-College, so I will take special care throughout this book not to talk down to you. I won't tell you that I had it worse, or that what you're going through is no big deal. On the contrary, the issues you face after you graduate—which are more intense in today's hectic society than they were when your parents went through them—are complex and frustrating. They deserve not to be blown off or ignored, but dealt with, understood, and even used as a launching pad for success. So while I am no longer a recent graduate, I do have a fond appreciation for post-graduate life. In addition, I have such an understanding of the issues many young adults face and a passion to help them . . . hence, this book.

So consider me a friend, an older sister who listens and doesn't solely dispense wisdom based on what I went through. Sure, I'll enlighten you with a few horrifying and hysterical tales as you read the book. I'll even give you some advice. But rest assured, it comes from a place of support rather than one that dismisses what you're going through. That's why you're not getting a book chock full of my opinions. Instead, I've collected stories about common issues that recent graduates faced so you can *identify* with them in hopes of resolving your own issues and making life during this somewhat tumultuous time just a little bit easier. You're not on your own. The After-College can be difficult. I've gathered people to tell you about it because if you can anticipate it, you can deal with it more effectively. That way, it won't hit you like a ton of bricks.

The Weight of it All

Let's not blame college for the quarterlife crisis or The After-College. I did that upon graduation because I didn't know any better. I thought a college degree was my ticket to happiness and financial security. When I started experiencing confusion over my career, for example, I thought that I should have been better prepared and blamed college for not being ready. Let me say now that Stockton had a great career center. I was the one who didn't take advantage of it. As I said, I was very busy with my life on campus. I was consumed with Circle K during my senior year, because I had finally risen to the head of the organization. My mind wasn't in the future-thinking place. I was living in the "now" back then, and in some ways, that wasn't a bad thing. In fact, that's why I have so many great memories of college—there was no pressure or worry; I was just going along doing my thing, kind of like childhood when you're fearless and carefree. Do I wish I had taken the initiative to get ready for the working world a little though? Absolutely. But that wouldn't have made life after college a breeze either.

Why do we, as young adults, put so much weight on getting a college degree and subsequently set ourselves up for disappointment when it doesn't come with a fabulous job and a shiny car? Think about it: Do you remember how much you put into just getting *into* a school? If you're like most graduates, getting to college wasn't easy. Whether it was academics or just trying to afford school, the fact that you survived and got your degree was no easy feat. Naturally, you want your reward. In my opinion, the *degree* is the reward—a great *career* is a possibility. Once you get the degree, you've got to *work* for the career. Not many people realize that!

I realize that I'm extremely career-focused. While family is important to me, I always knew—even when I thought that there could be nothing better than life on campus—that I wanted an enriching career. So when I came out with a degree in a field that interested me but couldn't personally fulfill my goals, that was a huge disappointment. I was disappointed in myself for having been so wrapped up in college life and not having prepared better for the future. *That was only four years,* I thought to myself, *this is forever!* I wanted to use my degree because I invested so much in it, and I wanted to apply my major to my job goals because, well, the major was "Environmental Studies." This was my first blunder. I thought that I had to get a job in the environmental sector. No wonder I didn't think there was anything better than college when I graduated—I thought I was doomed to a career in a field that I didn't even want to enter!

Okay, let me say that I wasn't altogether unprepared. I knew that I needed a resume. I knew how to find jobs. I was a decent public speaker, so I figured interviewing wouldn't be so hard. I could get a job. But I expected to march right into a career and be instantly gratified. Another false expectation. Everyone has to pay his or her dues at entry-level jobs. While they may not be terribly exciting, you can learn a great deal from them.

For me, finding my way career-wise was definitely the biggest hurdle of my After-College. But to be honest, I think that college can only give us so much. It gives you the Bachelor of Arts or Bachelor of Science on your resume that makes you qualify for a job. The rest is up to you. Students don't typically spend a lot of time learning about what life as a professional will be like (aside from a mandatory internship). For me, preparing included perusing a few books about the economic and professional climate. Most students do not obtain their degrees and gaze out to the horizon, feeling well-equipped to make it in the world. Some do . . . but not without feeling like they did that first day of kindergarten when they were dropped off and left in a strange environment.

My point is this: you can't blame everything that isn't what you hoped it would be as a recent college graduate on the school or the concept of attending college. When you define college as somewhere you go to prepare for the real world, you kind of set up a false expectation. While a *degree* gives you the requirement to succeed in the real world, that's about *all* it gives you. You must keep in mind that the rest of your time at college was spent enjoying yourself, making friends, falling in love, participating in campus life and learning about your course of study. At the time you're a student, the "real world" is so far off that it's normal not to be sitting in a dorm room each night learning strategies to use in dealing with an under-appreciative boss or teaching yourself how to balance paying rent with affording a social life. That's why The After-College is a harsh wake-up call—you are thrust from the land of the free into the working world, and you think it will be okay because you have your shiny new degree. It will, rest assured, but it's not a piece of cake. The truth is, you'll probably start out in an entry-level job that doesn't satisfy you and pays . . . well, not as great as the salary report in *Forbes* said it would. *This* is what makes your 20s so difficult: the expectations you have for yourself and emotions associated with them when life falls short of what you thought it would be like. On top of a major life transition, recent graduates are trying to deal with the fallout from expectations gone astray.

So, is that what you have to look forward to? Kind of. But let me say this: While you may not get what you expected as a recent graduate, knowing that life won't be picture perfect will help you immensely as you deal with that not-so-cool job, try to find a place of your own or attempt to keep a college flame going across the miles. Knowing that it's okay for your 20s to be rough—and that they're supposed to be—will help more than I can tell you. You'll know what to anticipate, and you'll feel more in control if things don't go as you planned—instead of feeling like the ground you firmly stood on your whole life was cruelly ripped out from beneath you. Expectations and perceptions have everything to do with surviving and thriving in The After-College.

The phase of your life you are about to enter will not be easy. Now you know that. Before we talk about how to deal with life as a new graduate, and how to flourish as a recent grad, let's look at what some 20-somethings had to say about their expectations. You'll see that it's normal to think of a degree as a cure-all, and you'll see that while it is not—and there are things college should have taught you—you can draw upon the experiences of others to find solace in this unpredictable, thrilling and wonderful time of your life.

What College Can't Prepare You For

Okay, so maybe college didn't prepare you for life in the real world. But there are also things you experience in life that college *cannot* prepare you for. Sure, I should have taken the career center up on their skill set assessment. I could have done a few things to ensure that I'd have had my first real job in May, instead of six months later in October. But in the place I was while I was still enrolled in school, I didn't see a career hunt as a priority—and I have to stop blaming myself for that. *Getting over the guilt of things like not being better prepared and not going into your degree field will help ease the transition into The After-College.*

Eventually, I came out of my After-College and my quarterlife crisis. I stopped blaming Stockton and started appreciating it again. I came to the realization that I couldn't have stayed longer and that it wasn't the school's fault—that was just life! I also realized that I didn't want to forget my early- and mid-20s. I wanted to make the most out of them, just like I did when I entered high school and college. I learned that I had to make do with what I had, and what I had wasn't so bad. At the end of the day, I *had* a college degree. I was an effective leader. And I had an exceptional sense of creativity. Even though I wasn't sure what I wanted to do with these things, I still *had* them. I still *had* my memories and friends too. It was time to move forward—I just couldn't deal with the pain of looking back and the shame of looking away anymore. There was no way to leave college and not feel the effects of the transition. Life is about changing and growing, and The After-College was a part of those developments.

I hope that in reading this, you do take some time to assess what you want to do. But other than that, you can only figure out what you want to do by going out and *living* your life. While that may be confusing and painful at times, it's better to *live* it and *feel* it than to want to *forget* it.

I challenge you to join a new generation of college graduates. Forget the previous ones that silently suffered through the hardships of their 20s, and pay no mind to the overindulgent whiners that live on their parents' couches and complain about their circumstances. Welcome to life in The After-College. Sure, we realize that life after college can be a shocker. Heck, it can be a full-on crisis too. But we're embracing it. We're not going to stay mum about it, but we're not going to sulk during the hardships either. Instead, we're looking to others for support. We're taking risks but being practical and objective as well.

We're dreaming big. We're using this time of transition to grow and have fun along the way. They say that after graduation is "the time of your life." The truth is that you have to *make* it that way. Good news, friends—you can.

Seven Success Tips for College Graduates Entering the Professional World

by Andy Masters

Euphoria from cap-and-gown celebrations will quickly turn to real world culture shock for many college graduates this year. Certainly, landing a job is concern number one, but how will these young professionals fare once they begin their careers? Are they actually prepared for what lies ahead? Andy Masters, St. Louis author of the newly released book *Life After College: What to Expect and How to Succeed in Your Career*, offers several pieces of advice for college graduates to get their careers off to a great start:

1. Build a Relationship With Your Boss. Like it or not, no single individual has a greater impact on your career future than your direct supervisor. So, how do you get on their good side from the start? Managers want to feel that you truly care, and that you are "in it with them" as a team. Bring your boss solutions, not problems. Most managers have enough problems already. When a problem arises, take initiative to consider what alternatives are available. Don't just throw the problem on their desk and have them figure it out. At some point, they will expect you to figure out what the best plan of action is first, so they don't have to. Try to build a relationship with your boss. Ask them about their career path, and always ask your boss for advice on what you or the company could do better. Understand what is particularly important to them, and how you can assist in those areas. Offer to stay late for projects, even if they might not be your responsibility. While these things may sound obvious, many Americans rush out the door at 4:59 without even saying "Good night."

2. Display Professionalism and Maturity. Unfortunately, the immature stereotype of young professionals does present a common barrier to advancement. Often, how you respond to adversity in a situation defines your professional maturity. A young professional views a mistake as a catastrophe, while a mature professional considers it a bump in the road. A young professional is quick to blame others, while a mature professional takes responsibility, and asks how a team can work better together in the future. Many will be subjected to various forms of nega-tivity, personality conflicts, and arguing in the workplace. However, that shouldn't be the norm. There will always be differences of opinion on how best to do things in an organization, but they shouldn't escalate to confrontation. Try to maintain your composure at all times, and don't allow your emotions to get the best of you. Remember that profes-sionalism is also judged in written communication, such as memos, reports, and especially e-mails. Ultimately, tact, common sense, and rational adult conversation should reign.

3. Find a Mentor Within the Company/Industry. Take advice from someone who has succeeded, and they will help you succeed. Makes sense, doesn't it? Mentors can offer priceless advice you just can't gain from reading books. They can also help introduce you to up-per management, allowing you to get on the fast-track radar screen. Some companies sponsor structured mentor programs, as do many professional organizations. Be sure to investigate these options first. Otherwise, you must rely on a more informal method of finding a men-tor. You might believe these people are too busy, or too important to talk to you. However, most people want to share their secrets to suc-cess with someone who really wants to listen. Deep down, almost ev-eryone relishes having someone look up to them. They also under-stand mentoring helps contribute to the future success of the company by helping develop other young leaders. Besides, they probably had a mentor too.

4. Master Interpersonal Relations and Teamwork. Possessing so-cial, professional, and teamwork skills are more important than ever before. A recent Harvard University study found that for every firing due to failure to perform, there were two firings due to personality con-flicts and communication issues. However, working in a team environ-ment with a diverse atmosphere will be a major adjustment for recent graduates. Most collegians study, take tests, and complete assign-ments in a predominantly individual setting throughout their academic career. Further, the professional environment requires communication and teamwork with those of vastly different ages, cultures, and back-grounds. Working newcomers will also have to co-exist with different personality types, such as egomaniacs, rule-breakers, brownnosers, and the "bare-minimum-to-get-by" guy. This can be challenging and is another area where professionalism and maturity can be tested. At the end of the day, everyone is still supposed to be on the same team. If you continue to possess the attitude that someone else's problem is also your problem, you will ultimately gain the respect of co-workers, no matter what personality type they are.

5. Understand the Power of Networking. Everyone has heard the phrase, "it's not just what you know, it's who you know." This is statistically proven, as the latest studies show that 65% of jobs in this country are either directly or indirectly gained through networking and personal contacts. Beyond that, often such jobs are better opportunities with higher pay. Places to network can include, well, everywhere. There are professional/trade organizations, alumni groups, community groups, and online communities available for young professionals to pursue immediately. Perhaps the most important concept to understand is that networking isn't just about what other people can do for you. If you initiate how you can assist another person first, you will gain a following of people who will go out of their way to help you whenever the opportunity arises. Keep making new contacts, build relationships with those contacts, and have a system for organizing and keeping in touch with your contacts. Lastly, it is a small world, so try to keep your enemies to a bare minimum and NEVER burn bridges.

6. Undertake a Strategic Development Plan. It is never too early to start thinking about where your current job will take you. What options are available for your next jump? It's important to understand typical advancement paths from your position, and what training and development is needed for advancement. Ideally, your company should realize the importance of investing in and developing future leaders. Otherwise, you will have to take initiative to seek out such development plans on your own. Many college graduates are tired of learning, and they're relieved they never have to study anymore. However, the most successful leaders don't stop learning at age 22, and neither should you. Invest in yourself, and continually gain knowledge from colleagues, books, seminars, and professional organizations. Try to identify your niche or area of specialization within a company or industry that will be in demand in the future. You must then create your own strategic development plan and hold yourself accountable to it.

7. Avoid Dangerous Pitfalls. You may think that employee binder you receive your first day is just a pile of boring policies no one reads, but take heed. Thousands of young professionals are reprimanded each year for violations such as Internet and e-mail abuse. Unfortunately, honesty and ethical judgment pose a common challenge for young professionals as well, often brought on by the pressure to rise through the ranks. There could be temptations to mislead a customer to get one more sale, or hide a mistake from management. However, losing the trust of management could be the most damaging consequence to your career. Further, there are over 15,000 sexual harassment cases filed every year in this country. Often, the intent of the offender may not necessarily be malicious, but rather they may not comprehend what is appropriate in the workplace vs. a "night out at the clubs." It is imperative to understand the rules of the game, and abide by those rules, to avoid irreparable damage to your career from the start.

Andy Masters is the author of *Life After College: What to Expect and How to Succeed in Your Career*. His website for the book, the program, and resources is www.life-after-college.com.

CHAPTER 2
Moving Back Home

"Welcome home . . . sort of."

If you thought the night before you left for college was the last time that you'd be in your bedroom at home, you may have been mistaken. Plenty of new graduates have nowhere else to go after they leave school—so they move home. Returning home after you graduate is . . . well, awkward. Case in point: I had to do it. I was like most of my classmates who didn't have jobs lined up, and I didn't have a place to crash either. When I moved home after graduation, I found that something was different, even though I had visited plenty during my college years.

Luckily, my mother never hounded me when I stayed up late and slept in. I was babysitting while I looked for a real job, so I was making some money. But there are horror stories out there about recent grads and their parents, mainly because of all the changes that happen to students during college. The conflict comes because you're even more of an adult after you graduate, and your parents are probably expecting more from you. There's a stigma about adults living at home with their parents—even when you're 21 or 22 and may have never even held a job. Still, there's an invisible yet palpable pressure to be out on your own, earning a reputable wage.

Then there's the bedroom debacle, as in, yours may be a storage facility now. (Hey, if they shelled out tuition, your space can hold a few boxes, right?) Sometimes coming home after college can be environmentally unsettling because you don't have your own space. Or you may not have enough "social space," meaning your parents may want you to follow their rules when you're used to following . . . well, nobody's. All of these factors can make moving back home overwhelming for recent graduates. While some are lucky to have awesome relationships with their families, many can't deny that there are changes when you move back in. As more and more grads choose this living option (and many have little choice), it's important to learn how to live with the rents the second time around.

Adjusting to Home Life: Why is My Room a Storage Closet Now?

Upon my graduation, I didn't know a single friend who wanted to move home. After four wonderful years of living independently, all of my school friends reluctantly moved home. Sorry Mom and Dad, but it's true: Most of us just want to remain on our own. That's not to say that recent graduates want to be cut off from their families—quite the contrary. Many are close with their families and want to stay connected, if not physically close too. But somehow it is unlikely for the majority of graduates to want to move home. That's because most of us who went to school away from home are used to living on our own. And for those who saved room and board money by living home during college, it's really time to get out! But, as we'll learn, that's not possible for all grads.

After completing his Bachelor's degree in civil engineering at Michigan Technological University, Sean moved home with his father and stepmother. He was there for four months until he relocated for his job. He says that at first being away from home was a big adjustment, but as his college career progressed, he enjoyed being farther from home. That way, he was able to establish an identity on his own.

He lived in a dorm his first year of school and then lived with friends in an apartment until graduation. Sean grew up taking care of laundry and preparing his own meals, so he did the same when he moved home after school.

"I think that the largest adjustment is that when you were away at college you could set your own pace and not have to inform anyone of your schedule and you could stay up real late," says Sean, now married and employed as a project manager. "While they [his parents] treated me as an adult, I still had to obey their rules since I lived in their house."

Kelly, a graduate of University of Washington, lived at home while she attended college to study sociology. It wasn't until after graduation that she moved out—two months after, to be exact—to start an independent life. But here's the thing: Independent living doesn't have to mean you live far away. (I still live 10 minutes from my mother and went to school an hour away. It was, and still is, just the right amount of distance. We're close, so that's why I suppose I haven't fled the Garden State!) Kelly is very much like me, wanting liberty yet also desiring to stay close to her parents. "I moved 15 minutes away. I am very close to my family and want to remain very close," she says. Living on her own wasn't difficult either, as she's got a little Martha Stewart blood in her. "I am a big homebody, so I loved decorating, having plants, cooking, cleaning," she says. "It was really, really fun for me." It still is. She has all the independence she could ask for, and her parents are still just a short drive away. While Sean and Kelly's experience with living at home after college were positive, there are others that didn't go as smoothly.

Nagging Parents: Why Won't They Leave Me Alone?

Andrea, a graduate of the University of Dallas and the State University of West Georgia, returned home after completing her Bachelor's degree. She was living with her mother, but admits it wasn't going well. She says that she had grown accustomed to doing household chores and cooking when she wanted, instead of when her mother wanted her to. She just was not used to being told what to do. "My mother jumped right into her old role of parent–dictator. She began leaving me lists of things to do on a daily basis," recalls Andrea, who was paying rent and refused to abide by her rules. "We would argue and one day it escalated and I left to go and live with my grandmother." After completing her Master's degree, she got a job as a teacher and completed licensure to become a board-certified art therapist, which is what she's doing now. While things were tense after graduation, Andrea is proud to report that things have been patched up with her mother today. She actually purchased a home within a mile of her mother's, and the two often meet to spend time together. Andrea's story is special because it shows that rifts can be mended—but that the tensions brought by graduation are very real and can be very intense.

Home . . . Altered

Carrie recalls growing up in Indiana, a place she couldn't wait to escape. So when she graduated from high school, she took off. "My hometown was a black hole that seemed to suck the life right out of everyone who stayed there. I wanted to get far away," she says. So she went to school at Morehead State University in Kentucky. Like most students, she didn't want to move home to Indiana after completing her four years of college. She planned to stay in Kentucky but says job prospects in her college town dwindled.

So she trekked back home, but only for a year. "I wasn't where I was supposed to be," admits Carrie, who lived with her parents during part of her time home. She says it was difficult to adjust to being asked where she was going and when she'd be back, and it was also hard to find her old bedroom converted into an office and storage space. "I was offended at first, but what did I expect—a shrine of my things?"

In addition to that, it was a big awakening when she realized how much her relationship with her parents had evolved. They were very supportive, yet Carrie says there was still a shift in how they related to one another. "We had all changed. I had grown up, and they had become actual people to me and not just parents."

Many of my friends agree with me when we talk about growing up and say that we knew it was official we were grown-ups when we started seeing our parents as people. It sounds like a small breakthrough, but it's a huge "discovery."

What can be more awkward than moving home? Staying there temporarily and knowing it's only for a set amount of time. Or feeling like you're living in a hotel. Actually for some recent grads, even living at home with no get-out-of-jail-free date can feel like staying in a hotel. Sara, who graduated from Thiel College in Pennsylvania with her Bachelor's degree in 2005, moved home for about a month before she was married. "My parents had turned my old bedroom into a den with a fold-out couch and a computer," she recalls.

Sara says her parents were cool about letting her crash, but she admits that seeing her grown up was probably "weird" for them. "I'm an only child, so sometimes I think they still see me as their baby, especially my mom," she adds. Sara completed her Master's in 2006 and lived on the campus of Kent State University in Ohio with her husband, who at the time of publication was completing his Ph.D.

The Boomerang Nation

Elina Furman wrote the book on moving back home after college. No, seriously, she did! That's why I thought it was instrumental to have the author of *Boomerang Nation: How to Survive Living with Your Parents... the Second Time Around* speak out in this book. She coined the term "Boomerang Nation" to describe the nearly 18 million 18- to 35-year-olds who live at home with their parents. She says this rapidly growing phenomenon is becoming increasingly popular for graduates and young adults, and it is caused by the increased cost of living, weak job market, credit card debt, and excessive student loans. Furman reports that 63 percent of American college students plan to live at home after graduation. While it may not be their desired goal, moving back home is a very real deal for many recent grads.

"There are many factors today that are driving people's return to the nest," explains Furman, a graduate of the University of Illinois Champaign-Urbana, who currently resides in New York. "There's the return to historic immigration levels, increasing health care costs, the continued segmentation between the haves and have nots, rising costs of education, and predatory lending by credit card companies, just to name a few. Also, there are many emotional reasons why people move back home, including the breakup of a relationship or marriage and also as relief from some of the stresses of everyday life," she says. But Furman realizes that most graduates move home after school—whether being out on their own for a while or not—because of financial problems, including credit card debt. She moved home upon graduation, and not into the best scenario either. Her parents were in the middle of a complicated divorce. Needless to say, her living situation was not ideal, and she later moved with her mother and sister into a condo.

"My mom and I have always been close and I was very worried about her living on her own," recalls Furman. "As much as I thought that she would be scared living by herself, I realized I was even more nervous, and the same was probably true of my sister. So all three of us set off on the new adventure, more roommates and friends by now than nagging family members." Settled and on her own now, Furman is a survivor of the boomerang move back home.

As I've mentioned, I never wanted to move home after I left Stockton. While I had a great relationship with my family and still do, I wanted to be independent after graduation. At the time, there were very little positives in my life, but the thought of having my own apartment was extremely appealing. See? I became a Boomeranger too. Sure, it was only for six months, but if you've been there, you know that six months is long enough! Yet, for other grads, living at home isn't a drag at all—it all depends on the individual.

Furman wants people our age to know that there's no right or wrong reason to move home. "The only wrong reason would be if someone moved home to avoid taking responsibility for their life or because they didn't want to work anymore. Obviously, we all have to work to support ourselves."

So are Boomerangers a thing of the "now," or will the trend continue? Furman cites statistics from the U.S. Census: Generation Y is set to increase the number of people living at home by several million. Not only more Y'ers than X'ers, they have seen their older brothers and sisters move back home. As a result, they feel they will face less stigma if they choose to cohabitate with parents in their 20s and 30s.

Movin' In, Movin' Up—or Movin' Out?

Okay, let's face it: Moving home isn't that bad. Even if you have to pay some rent to your folks, living with them enables you to get on your feet (and raid the fridge late at night too). If you work while you are living at home, you'll probably be able to save some money. That's a huge benefit to living at home, because your friends who are living on their own are spending most of their income on rent and utilities. Furman agrees. "You can save money to achieve some financial landmarks earlier, e.g. buying a home, paying down your school loans and lessening your credit card debt," she explains. "For many people who choose not to move back home, it could take them significantly longer to achieve the same milestones." Furman adds that if the relationship between you and your parents or parent is strong, it's nice to have that built-in support system while you navigate The After-College. "I think at first it can be very scary to make the transition back home," she says. But once you get adjusted, you'll probably embrace it, especially if the relationship with your parent(s) is positive. Furman continues, "If it's good, it can make living at home significantly easier."

Of course, staying with the rents does have its disadvantages. Not all college students live away at school during college (another money-saver!) so they may not have the "shock" of moving home, but it can be a bummer to still be at home after college graduation. "Many of the Boomerangers I've interviewed report feelings of isolation, shame, and loss of self-esteem as a result of their lifestyles," Furman says. That's why she wanted to eliminate the stigma about living at home. Even though the statistics say that millions of young adults are nesting with their parents, Furman says there is still not enough information to bring awareness about the topic. At the time of this publication, she said that there wasn't a book on the market to help young adults cope with living at home for the second time around. "As a result, the majority of

Boomerangers are living in a virtual bubble, unaware that their life-styles so closely mirror those of their peers. They assume that they have failed, where everyone else has succeeded; that while they couldn't hack it in the real world, everyone else has thrived," she explains. Furman hopes that her message rings true for the millions of Boomerangers out there, and she wants to let them know that they are not alone. Many successful people have moved back home with their parents, and there are strategies to cope with that living scenario.

There is no right or wrong reason to move home, minus that whole mooching-off-the-rents thing. Aside from the stigma, it's important to look around you and look at just how many of your classmates *are* moving home. Probably plenty of them—at least right after graduation day. Furman suggests that grads ask themselves the following questions to determine whether they must move home or not:

- *Can you afford to live on your own?* If you can't, you may not have any other choice but to move home.

- *Do you have significant credit card debt?* If yes, it might be a good idea to move home and start paying down the balances.

- *Do you have a good relationship with parents?* If yes, this will make living at home significantly easier.

- *Where do your parents live?* If they live near or in a big city, you may have more opportunities for jobs and it will be easier to maintain a thriving social life.

Boomeranger or not, I think it's important to remember that there are advantages of moving home, just as there are benefits to living on your own. It's important to decide what is best for you, and to be practical at the same time. If you don't have a job lined up, for example, it's probably not the best time to look for an apartment. (Even if your parents offer to pay, you may not like living off their funds rather than your own.) If you're not looking forward to heading back home, keep reminding yourself that it's only temporary. You will be able to get your own place someday soon, and in many cases, relationships with family will improve upon moving out. (People can get *very* friendly when they see an outgoing U-Haul truck!)

On the reverse, some grads get a little too cozy at home, even if they are living in their old bedroom/family office/storage closet. "Boomerangers have to know when it's time to leave," Furman says. "It's very important to set a cut-off time because it's easy to make excuses and keep pushing off moving out. You know you're ready to leave when you've lined up a solid job, found an affordable living situation, are dying to get out of the house, and obviously if your parents have changed the locks."

Coping With Life at Home: The After-College Way

I asked Richard Marquis, an author, speaker and college success expert, to share some tips on moving back home after college. Richard runs the Michigan-based consultancy, Marquis Advantage (www. gradegrabbers.com) and has plenty of valuable advice for graduates heading back home after graduation.

What advice do you have for students who had to move home after school and face pressure from their parents and are feeling crowded after living on their own for four or more years?

Who wouldn't feel crowded? Three (or more) adults living under the same roof is difficult under the best of circumstances, even when no one is related. Like it or not, moving in with parents brings uniquely unavoidable pressures. Nevertheless, if you find yourself living with your parents after graduation, it may be helpful to keep the following three points in mind:

1. Take what they are doing for you as a favor. Whatever the reason you find yourself living with your parent(s), realize that they are doing you a big favor. They have agreed to helping you to make do by putting you up and (make no mistake about it) putting up with you too. Know that "house rules" apply. Never assume that you can run your parents' home like a dorm. They do not want you to bring friends over to get drunk, to raise the roof past midnight or to invite someone to stay overnight, etc.

2. Take it in stride. Things will get strained at times. It is then that your folks will hit you with the heavy artillery, such as: "I remember you when you were loading your diapers!" Regardless of what agreements you have worked out, nerves will fray. That said, it may be helpful to bear in mind that this living arrangement is only temporary. It is also valuable to see things from their perspective from time to time. After all, it was probably not so crowded for them until you moved back in. Of course, it can be aggravating when parents ask, "Where are you going?" or "What are you doing today?" or, even worse, "What are we all doing tonight?" If you can take it in stride, so much the better. But the day will come when it is time to move on to the next point.

3. Take off as soon as you are able. There will come a time when you must extend sincere thanks for all of their help and finally leave the roost. However difficult the circumstances were during your stay, do your best to leave on good graces. You owe them a lot. They put up with raising you for years, didn't they? Be sure to thank them. Their intention was never to crowd you out but to help you out. When it's time to part company, they hope you will have been helped and that you will love them—regardless. Leave it at that.

GET YOUR FACTS STRAIGHT

By Elina Furman, Author of *Boomerang Nation: How to Survive Living with Your Parents...the Second Time Around*

Myth: College graduation marks the beginning of domestic and financial independence.
Fact: Sixty-three percent of U.S. college students plan to live at home after graduation.

Myth: Boomerangers are always a financial burden on their families.
Fact: About 50 percent of Boomerangers contribute to household rent and expenses.

Myth: Living at home is a sign of failure.
Fact: Twenty-five percent of the Boomerang population is attending a post-secondary institution, and 45 percent are working full time (Mitchell, 1998).

Myth: The return home is a temporary, one-time event.
Fact: Some families reported kids who boomeranged three or more times. Half of young adults return within 30 months, often with a spouse or child back in tow (Snyder, 2000).

Myth: Parents are always unhappy with having to change their lifestyle.
Fact: Seventy-three percent of parents (Mitchell and Gee, 1998) reported being "very satisfied."

Myth: The Boomerang phenomenon will decrease over time.
Fact: As Generation Y reaches adulthood, there will be more 20- to 34-year-olds in 2010 than in 2000, increasing the number of Boomerangers (U.S. Census Bureau).

Reprinted with permission from Elina Furman at www.boomerangnation.com.

CHAPTER 3
Living On Your Own

"Free at last!"

I t's no wonder that so many graduates want to live on their own after college—many of us who lived on campus want to continue our freedom, and those who stayed at home during college are ready to fly the coop. But when you do get your own place after college—alone or with roommates—it can be quite an awakening. There is rent to pay, an apartment to clean and maybe a roommate to mesh with. In addition, you're responsible for getting your meals and making sure you manage your time effectively so work doesn't suffer.

My first apartment was a refurbished motel room. It had a kitchen, living room, bedroom, and bathroom, and it only cost $400 a month because it was a winter season rental. In its defense, it was right across the street from the beach. I got this apartment shortly after I got my first real job. The *only* reason I was able to move out was because of the insanely cheap rent. Most grads don't have it this lucky, and I realize that. Getting your own place—no matter what it's like or how much it costs—is a huge part of The After-College. You'll find that your first apartment in the real world is much different than life on campus. Even though you were "on your own" then, this is a little different.

Boosting Your Relationship with the Rents— Move Out!

Emily, who moved five hours from home to attend Boston University, says she enjoyed living on her own during college. "I had a loving, good home, but I was so overprotected that getting away from the suburban bubble was absolutely essential," she says. "I loved living away from home. My relationship with my parents and younger brother improved and I learned to be independent and trust myself in ways I never could before," Emily adds. At the time of publication, Emily was still living in her college apartment. "My parents are paying for it until I have a job. I pay my utilities and all personal expenses and they know I'm trying my best to find employment, so they don't mind putting up with a few more months of rent, which is very generous," she explains. "I don't like having to rely on them and I am dying to be able to pay my rent, but I'm still stuck in this weird limbo until I can get a job."

Emily notes that money is a limiting factor in just about everything. While she says she doesn't care about driving a flashy car or earning millions, she often hears that she is young and free and can travel the world. "Of course, I can't! It's only people with money who can do that. I'd move to another city, but I can't afford to. I'd stop worrying about things, but I can't afford to," she adds. While money may be an issue now, Emily is physically living on her own in her alma mater city.

Kristen didn't feel the sting of living away at home after college. She went to University of Mary Washington in Virginia, about 300 miles from her home in New Jersey. She didn't visit home much while she was attending school. "It felt like I moved out as soon as I started college," explains Kristen. She went home for two summers and then lived with her now-husband. "Once I got to Fredericksburg, Virginia where my college is located, it felt more like home than anywhere else I'd ever been. Now I live outside the city, but I still go there several times a week just to hang out and meet up with friends."

Emery, a graduate of Florida International University, lived at home until her last semester as an undergraduate. As a graduate student at the same college, she did move to a nearby efficiency apartment but says she didn't move far from home and her school due to the high costs. Thankfully, Emery says her parents seem to have more respect for her since she moved out. "They still call me almost everyday to check on me and remind me of this and that," says Emery. "But they let me be, which is what I wanted. When we visit [now], we actually communicate better and spend quality time together, unlike before."

Most recent grads say that the relationship they have with their families tends to improve with a little space. It's kind of that whole thing about absence making the heart grow fonder. I have found—and this has been reinforced by several interviewees in this book—that once grown children move out, things seem less tense between them and their parents. This is probably because they aren't under the same roof all the time. They can talk when they want. The awkwardness associated with living at home was removed.

The discomfort of boomeranging home after college graduation is caused not only by the interaction with our families when we're all crammed into one structure, but also because we are thinking of what we should be doing instead of being back at home. You feel out of place, and it places a strain on your family relationships. But as you'll hear throughout the course of this book, the shoulds are the expectations that can lead to a 20-something meltdown. The shoulds are those unseen, unstated metrics that we measure ourselves against. The shoulds are what can make The After-College a living hell if we let them. It's nice to think that you have a job lined up before you put on your cap and gown, and that this instant dream career will comfortably pay rent for a cushy apartment. But it's really not so practical. It can take a while to get on your feet, and it may not be walk down the path that you'd like. This is what The After-College is all about—finding your own way when you have no clue where you're going.

Consider another reason that you may feel "weird" to be back at home: you are back where you started! It may seem that you have taken a step backwards to where you were when you graduated high school.

You thought that a degree meant a job and an apartment, so it can feel disorienting to be back in your old room, (which, in many cases, is now used for storage). Living in a temporary-looking setting can be quite unnerving too. In addition, uncomfortable feelings can stem from being on your own so long, and then a move back home makes you feel trapped. When I was away at school, my mother certainly never knew when I got in at 3 a.m., or when I engaged in what she might consider "debauched" activities. At home, your family is there watching your every step. They may want you home at a certain time. They may nag you about going out with friends if you don't have a job. They may tell you to do housework instead of sitting on the couch. This can lead to fights and tense relationships. That is when more uncomfortable feelings emerge—when you feel like it's not really your home anymore. That's also usually when you finally leave.

Actor Zach Braff's character Andrew Largeman in the film *Garden State* was spot on when he described moving home after school and realizing that it wasn't *his* home anymore. In the movie, he told Natalie Portman's character that she would see what it meant when she moved out. He said realizing his home wasn't his anymore just sort of happens one day, and when it does, you can never get your home back. To create a new sense of home, you have to make it by establishing and settling into your own place. He tells her that he thinks the concept of family is just a bunch of people who miss a "home" that doesn't exist. If you've seen this movie and recall this scene, you know how profound it was. While home may feel gone, you know it isn't—that in most cases, you can always go home to your parents' house. It may not feel the same though. This is part of growing up, a phase of The After-College. Part of the excitement and part of the healing you'll undergo from grieving your "loss of home" is that you get to make your own home and your own life. That can be pretty cool.

Breaking Ties

Sometimes students move away from home because of family issues. So when they break free, it feels especially fabulous. Rebecca, an Indiana University graduate, says she chose to go far from home for college, and it was a "dream come true." In fact, getting away was a big draw to attend college. "My home life was awful as a child, and most of my high school friends were going nowhere fast," she says. "At school, I met new friends who respected my wishes not to drink, and they had similar goals, as I did, to graduate."

Upon getting her degree, Rebecca chose not to move back home due to poor family relationships. "I didn't really have a home to move to, due to some serious family issues," explains Rebecca. She moved about two hours away from her hometown, which she still affiliates with bad memories. But the new arrangement works for her. "I live close enough that I can go visit whenever I want, but far enough away that my family will call before they drop by and they respect my time."

With an undergraduate degree in art, Rebecca hasn't been able to find a lot of work in her field and currently is employed at a car dealership while trying to pursue art on the side. Rebecca maintains that people should only get degrees if they know what they want to do with them. "Going to college is so expensive, and it doesn't guarantee anything. I'll be paying off my student loans until I'm 40, but I don't know if my degree will ever increase my income," she says. "My first job out of school was stapling, filing and answering the phone. I could have done that with a second grade education!"

While Rebecca hasn't found work within her field, I believe that her college education will be a plus for her—just as I believe it is for others. Even if you don't know what you want to do, getting a degree is never a waste. If you apply it, you'll find that you will have more career opportunities. Sure, Rebecca might have been able to perform the duties of her first job without a degree—but she couldn't have moved up without that first job, and most companies won't hire you for a job like that without a degree. So in the long run, having a degree will probably pay off for Rebecca.

Now married, Rebecca has been prudent with her money, and she says she ate a lot of macaroni and cheese and ramen noodles to ensure she had enough money to continue living away from home. Her father has been somewhat supportive, but she has not been able to rely on her mother for financial assistance. But in speaking with Rebecca, I got the idea that her freedom was well worth chowing down on inexpensive carbs.

For Melissa, a graduate of Spring Arbor University in Michigan, it wasn't so much her family as it was a lack of job opportunities that caused her to move away from home. After her parents divorced, Melissa took stock of her situation. "I lived in a small town and to get to any major college in the nearby areas, I was looking at a long drive. Also, being in a small town, there was very little opportunity to find a job. I was put into a situation where I pretty much had to take care of myself, my own expenses, and my own education. Looking back, I really wish that I had stayed around home a lot longer, perhaps spending the first couple of years in one of the local community colleges," recalls Melissa. Even if the divorce hadn't happened, Melissa says she doesn't think she would have stuck around too long because the region lacked decent job opportunities.

The High Price—Literally—of Living on Your Own

As cool as it may be to have your own place, rent can be expensive. I specifically remember walking into a realty office while searching for my first apartment. The agent told me that my rent should equal one week of my pay. I looked at her, astonished. While at the time, the rent for my first apartment (the converted motel room on the beach) was only $400, that was just a little more than a week's take-home pay. To this day, I still think about that "rule." Sure, I have heard it since then many times, but I find it highly impractical. I don't think many grads would get apartments if they were waiting for a week's take-home salary to equal their rent. Rents can be exorbitant. Many grads report feeling like they're holding down a job solely to pay the rent—especially in major metropolitan areas where prices tend to be higher.

I got lucky with inexpensive rent at my first apartment. Since I made about $1,100 a month, you'd probably figure that I had plenty of money left over for everything. Not so! Monthly, I was paying about $250 in credit card debt, $115 in school loans, $60 for electric and heat, $50 for water, $60 for a cell phone, $20 for a land line, $45 for cable and about $200 for food. This left little for needless spending, let alone saving. So before you rush out to get an apartment, crunch the numbers. Better yet, get a roommate. It's a great way to be out on your own while reducing the cost of living. Living expenses can be much more than what's owed monthly on a lease!

Jessica moved about 500 miles from her home in Scotland just to attend college. Upon graduation from the Mountview Academy for the Performing Arts in London, she stayed in the city for a few years. "I had always wanted to live in London and didn't want to go home after I finished my studies, not only because I never really felt at home in Scotland but also because the majority of job opportunities in theatre and television were in London." But living in the big city wasn't easy. Accommodations were very pricey, and where they weren't? . . . Well, that's where Jessica wound up. She first stayed in a one-room apartment in a converted hotel in Walthamstow, East London, which cost about $100 a week plus utilities.

"The area was extremely violent and rough. The apartment next door to me was broken into the day before I moved my things in, people looking for drug money, and the rumor was that the previous tenant in my room had run away from the same gangs," Jessica recalls. "A full-scale gang fight took place a few days after I'd been living there." It wasn't soon before she moved to Northern London and got an apartment closer to her school for $550 a month. "There was very little chance of going somewhere else though, so I had to make do and did make the most of the place. I stayed there after graduation and most of my wages went into paying the rent." While she didn't mind living in London, Jessica did eventually move back home after inheriting a one-bedroom apartment in Glasgow, Scotland, "simply because it was too difficult for me to change jobs or find a career I liked because of the pressure of maintaining that rent," she concludes.

Money is certainly a factor for all of the people I interviewed. Even when they got out into their own places and obtained well-paying jobs, rent was the huge money-eater. While I know it's nice to be independent, getting a roommate can often be a smart choice.

I wanted to stay on my own after six months in a winter rental but did not have the financial resources to afford living there year-round. Luckily, a coworker was looking to move into her landlord's three-bedroom unit, and we managed to swing the rent together for $550 apiece, including utilities. I certainly was blessed, and realize (especially after hearing Jessica's tale) that not all grads had the luck of the draw like I did with my safe location. While having a roommate was financially practical, I do look back fondly on my six months of living alone.

Going the Martha Route

Some graduates find that maintaining their apartments while living away from their parents' home is quite the challenge. Emery, the graduate of Florida International University that I told you about earlier, works 9 a.m. to 5 p.m. most days and attends graduate school in the evenings. She says she usually eats out at a restaurant or prepares something easy for meals. "Taking care of the apartment around my schedule was hard," she explains. "I had no time to clean as well as I'd have liked to."

Jessica didn't have a problem taking care of food preparation in her London pad. "I had cooked for myself since I was in high school, as my parents both worked and were not at home a lot of the time," she explains. But while cooking wasn't a problem for her, affording food was. "Being in London, food and supplies were also much more expensive than where I grew up, and the shops in my area were mostly small delicatessen-style places that charged a fortune for simple groceries," she recalls. When it came to taking care of her place, she did struggle to clean and maintain her apartment. "The structure of the place was extremely old and not very well cared for, so we had water streaming down the walls every time it rained (which in this country was practically all year) and the windows were so old and crusty that they didn't all open," she adds.

Jessica utilized the theater carpentry and painting skills she used in college. "I tried my best to smuggle out a few supplies from our theatrical productions to tidy the place up, but the renovations usually didn't last," she says. With 13 other tenants in the building, most there only temporarily, it was hard to find anyone interested in helping to take care of the place.

Leah, a University of New Hampshire graduate, said she never minded cooking but was shocked to see how much groceries cost. She started doing her own grocery shopping when she moved to Boston with a group of friends within three months of graduating. "It is hard to cook for one person," she says. "I eat by myself a lot because all of us had different schedules and making food for one is time consuming and creates a lot of leftovers," Leah says. While finding time to eat together can be hard, snagging her apartment was not. "I really like the apartment we moved into. We found it in the suburbs of Boston where rent was a little cheaper but access to the city was still close. Now I have lived here for almost a year and have a more steady income so in August one of my roommates and I will be moving even closer to the city. It wasn't hard to find someplace affordable. We searched using Craigslist and were able to find exactly what we wanted," she adds.

For me, home domestics became something I enjoyed. Like many recent grads, when I moved to my first apartment I had to call my mother for tips on how to cook. As I grew more skilled at keeping a nice home and wanting to make it better, I learned how to take care of my place. Most graduates—males or females—don't move into an apartment and know instantly how to make fabulous dinners. (Plus, when you're cooking for one, what's the point of getting fancy?) But you can make an effort to eat well, keep the apartment clean and perhaps even get a houseplant or a pet. I think you'll find that once you have a place of your own, you'll enjoy tailoring it to match your lifestyle. And if you're not domestically gifted, you can call on your parents, an older sibling or another adult in your life for advice. My mother got plenty of panicky calls about what to do with a burning roast or a clogged toilet. She was great in helping me—another thing that strengthened our bond.

The Curse of the Strange Roommate and Other Dreadful Living Tales

While Leah has it good with her roommates, other grads haven't been as lucky. From lopsided apartments to bizarre roommates, living arrangements can be a little weird sometimes, mostly because you're living on the low-income scale, which many of us aren't used to. Clean laundry and home-cooked meals are no longer readily available, and you've got to do it all yourself. You won't believe how hard it is to afford all the luxuries that you've taken for granted. (Even cafeteria food can be considered a luxury if you have no clue how to prepare meals upon moving out!)

Because it's cheaper to share a pad with someone, a lot of recent college graduates combine resources and share living quarters, but when you have to do so with someone you don't know, you can't just call the residence life office for a roommate switch like you could have back in school.

Cathleen, a graduate of Fordham University, moved home for a few weeks and then into an apartment in Hoboken, New Jersey. With an easy commute into New York City (without paying the exorbitant rent) it seemed like a good choice. "I checked the town paper every week for apartments to rent. It became obvious that it would be too expensive to live on my own so I took an apartment with a strange girl," recalls Cathleen, an arrangement that didn't work out at all. Cathleen believes that she was prepared for the domestic challenges of living alone, but not for the somewhat obsessive roommate with which she found herself paired. On top of that, the floor plan of their apartment was such that in order for her roommate to get to her bedroom, she had to walk through Cathleen's. Yeah, it was that bad. But Cathleen learned to cope with the unfavorable living situation. In fact, she sums it up by saying, "At least now I know I can live anywhere if I need to!" What a positive comment on a seemingly not-fun-at-all living arrangement.

Kristen and her beau found a great apartment in an old home about 20 minutes from school. Perfect, right? Nope. "A week before we were supposed to move in, the house was condemned!" Kristen explains.

Fortunately, the pair found another pad close to school the very next day. They're currently married and just bought a house. "But for the 24 hours we didn't know where we were going to live, we were freaking out."

My husband once lived in a house that was literally crooked. He had some good times there. The rent was inexpensive, and by combining his financial resources with that of a roommate, he remembers the years fondly. We always get a giggle remembering when we'd have parties there and the guests would ask, "Is it me, or is your ceiling tilting down?"

And yes, I had my own awkward living situation. After moving out of the "motel" and in with a roommate, I soon realized that she wasn't at all as I had perceived her. Sure, Kim was bubbly and fun to hang around with, but I didn't know she was like that all the time. Up at about 6 a.m. every day and not back into bed until 2 a.m. the following morning, I soon found that she was a little too friendly for my tastes. Case in point: I woke up one day and discovered a cop passed out on my couch. He was just one of several strangers that I found in my house over the year Kim and I lived together. One day I was driving through town and was pulled over by a patrolman. The officer gave me a ticket and went back to his car to file the report. When he walked back to my car and handed me the ticket, I looked more closely at him. I asked his first name and then realized he was my roommate's one-night stand! He recalled seeing me at the apartment and said he wouldn't have issued me a ticket had he known that I was Kim's roommate! So I did have a roommate who got around town. Too bad I was so annoyed with her networking or I could have saved myself a court date!

Living situations in your 20s are truly unique. Even though you work at a Fortune 500 company, no one needs to know that your pantry is only filled with ramen noodles and that you sleep on an aero bed. Of course, eventually you'll have to part with neon signs in your apartment window and a beer pong table in the dining room, but for now you can enjoy it. After all, if Joey and Chandler played foosball in the kitchen, you can too.

CHAPTER 4
Major Confusion

"I paid $50,000 a year for what?"

It happens to the best of us. You go to college thinking that it is a step in the right direction. And it is—although sometimes what you study during those four years leaves you with *no* direction, even though you think it should have. So it goes . . . another graduate enters the world with absolutely no interest in using his or her college degree. Who can blame someone for not knowing how to apply a degree in Russian literature or philosophy (or in my case, environmental studies) to today's corporate climate? Sometimes graduation is like taking the blinders off. You study for so long that you can't see what you want to do with your life until it's time to make money and fend for yourself. In other cases, graduates cannot find a job in their degree fields and they are forced to take jobs in other industries. Others do not strive to get a job where a college degree is a requirement. In all three of these cases, not using—or not being able *to* use—one's degree can be yet another frustration piled onto 20-somethings during The After-College.

In these circumstances, college graduates need to explore other opportunities. When graduates are thrown into these predicaments, it can feel like the supposed "most exciting" time of their lives is a spiral down into a pit of hopelessness. When you're in your early 20s and you've spent so much time in school, what are you to do when you can't apply what you've learned—or you don't even want to try? It makes many recent graduates wonder what life is all about (and it's perfectly natural to speculate!).

Anna Ivey, an admissions and career counselor based out of Massachusetts, says that while liberal arts majors do not "use" their majors in the working world (in the sense that they don't have jobs in the archeology, history, or English literature fields, for example) they do gain broader, more transferable skills that can readily be used such as writing, speaking, and critical thinking. "I recently met a woman who had majored in Art History and now works in psychopharmacology," says Ivey. "She went off and earned two Ph.D.s in subject areas that had nothing to do with her undergraduate major. Good liberal arts training keeps a lot of doors open."

On the other hand, pre-professional college majors are more likely to end up in jobs related to their majors, whether that's business, accounting, communications, pre-med, or engineering. "Even those majors, however, teach transferable skills (quantitative analysis, case analysis, optimization and design, coding, systems, etc.)," Ivey notes. "These days, it's impossible to predict what kind of career someone is going to have. Jobs change, technology upgrades, the economy shifts, specializations come and go, and personal preferences change, so it's best to focus on developing broader, transportable skills rather than planning on working within a narrow niche for the rest of time." Not directly applying your degree in the field you studied? Whether you want to or not, it's not uncommon to wind up in a completely different field, where you can find yourself completely fulfilled. "College students need to plan on reinventing themselves many times over the course of their careers," Ivey advises.

I should also add that just because you don't directly apply your degree in the field you studied doesn't mean that you aren't using your degree. I write everyday about topics that don't include the environment—or science. But I know I'm using my college degree. I personally went from being a science major to a writer, so I know all about getting a degree that you don't want to use. I also know that it's hard when you can't get a job in your degree field and that it can be confusing when you don't want a job that even requires a college degree. Regardless what your reasons are for not going into the field of your major, hopefully you can find some solace in this chapter and some ideas to help you be at peace if you cannot directly apply your degree temporarily or permanently. For many, getting over the fact that you won't work in the field that you studied can be a huge let down. (It was in my case, even though I had no interest in science. I still felt that it was what I should have been doing.) It took me a long time to give myself permission to do what I loved instead. No one said it was okay not to get a job in the science field. No wonder I struggled so much with my career during my After-College.

Four or more years ago, you may have had a major of "undecided" or "undeclared." This means that at the time, you were a student who could not state definitively what you wanted to study. Perhaps you may now not know what you want to do. In other words, you may just be what I call an "Undecided Graduate," which means that you have a college degree but you're not sure what the heck it is that you want to do. Trust me, you will figure it out. Just like you had two years in college to declare a major, you've got some time before you really need to buckle down in a career field (if you ever really do need to settle at all!).

First, it's okay if your first job doesn't live up to your expectations. The point is to get your feet wet. If you're in a gig that you despise, you will find a better one. Second, don't give up on your career or enter graduate school as a means to run away from entering the working world. Finally, even if you don't use your degree, you can still find meaningful work and benefit from having spent time earning that degree.

Now let's explore how to deal with not directly applying your college certification—whether it's intentional or not.

Your First Job is Just a Job

While everyone dreams of starting that ideal career the day after graduation, few are lucky enough to do so. Ask any successful person what their first job was and you'll get answers that range from the ordinary to the horrible. For example, actor Nicholas Cage sold popcorn at a movie theater, and singer Bon Jovi was a Christmas tree decoration maker. And did you know that Oprah Winfrey got a job as a reporter for a radio station after stopping in to pick up a watch she won on the air during a contest? These jobs didn't get in the way of these celebrities' achievements. They're proof that you may have to get a little butter or glitter on your hands, but you can move out of a dead-end job should you have to take one.

Robert, a graduate of Plymouth State University in New Hampshire, moved home with his parents after receiving his degree in English Literature. He says he could not do much with his degree other than teach, and he could not find a teaching job fresh out of college. Like many graduates in similar situations, he also thought about going to graduate school. For now, he is working in a bookstore around works of literature, but it is not ideally what he had hoped to be doing.

"Right now, I don't think I'll ever get in and do what it is I want to do with my life," says Robert, who admits struggling with feelings of panic and depression. He says his current job is "horrible." He's looking for a new gig but is struggling to find one. I have faith that he will get to wherever he wants to be if he tries. At least for now, he can pay the rent while he's looking for something better. It's okay to have a job outside your field, or a job like one you had in high school, for a while. Heck, if you really want to, you can do that for the rest of your life . . . because it's your life.

That's what I had to do for a while—go back to my college job. I babysat for six months before getting my first "real" job. Actually I had good instincts coming out of college when I decided that I didn't want to use my environmental science degree. I needed something I knew how to do and figured writing was a natural gift (but didn't think it was anything that would help me to make a living). I got a job as a reporter at a weekly newspaper and moved to a daily publication six months later. So you could say even though I didn't apply my educational specialization to my degree field right away, I knew what I wanted to do straight out of college . . . sort of. Although I'd always dreamed of being an author, I never considered becoming a writer. Like Robert, I got a job that paid the bills and exposed me to just about everything—politics, human interest topics, and current events. For me, it was a smart move and a great stepping stone.

Then came an intense period of self-doubt. I felt guilty for not even trying a job in the environmental industry. That's when I figured that a jaunt in the environmental business would help me decide if I was really meant to write. (I could not comprehend going from a degree in the left-brained field to a career in the right-brained artistic world.) I wasn't ready to get into the mud as an entry-level environmental technician either, so I took a job in communications for an environmental firm. After two years there, I realized what I knew somewhere deep inside when I came to my career—I was meant to write. Better yet, I knew that I didn't want to slave away at a job like I had at the time, which had no room for advancement. Plus, I wanted to be involved in all industries and learn new things, as I did when I was a journalist. But one thing was for sure: I knew I didn't want to go back to writing for a newspaper.

I wound up leaving my job at the environmental company and editing another daily newspaper. It was the perfect gig to help me get enough money to pay bills and to be able to build my dream business on the side. My copywriting venture took off solidly and steadily, and it gave me the freedom, enjoyment and money to pursue book writing. I was making good money writing marketing collateral for companies, and soon after I started, the self-doubt over "what do I want to do with my life" dissipated. So I guess you could say that we can arrive at our destiny if we follow our hearts—even when we need to prove to ourselves that our hearts are in the right place to begin with.

The Temp Route

Sometimes when you want to use your college education, you simply can't—at least right away—as Robert's story illustrated. That also was the case with Samantha, who graduated from Bethel College in Minnesota with a degree in professional and creative writing.

"The day before I graduated, I insisted to my dad that I was going to be an artist and was never going to work an office job," recalls Samantha. A few months later, she knew that taking an office job was necessary to pay off her student loans, and getting a writing job was difficult. She went through a temp agency and got a job as a receptionist.

While most of her friends were trying to make a living with their art, she was the only one holding down a "real job." She says her friends didn't look down on her for it, though a few were jealous she was financially stable enough to enjoy living. "I have been doing office work ever since and don't regret it at all," says Samantha, who is currently working in the financial industry and applying her communications skills. "I do my creative stuff in my 'spare time' and it makes for a great balance."

Switching Focus

In my case, I didn't want to use my degree—I knew that collecting soil samples as a field technician for an environmental company wasn't my passion. Knowing I wanted to write, I simply changed gears. Of course, I felt a lot of personal guilt for doing so until I developed confidence in my abilities. The point here is that it's okay to follow a different career path than the one you selected for yourself when you were most likely still attending pep rallies during high school. There were many changes that you experienced personally and professionally as you made your way through college, and now in The After-College, it is normal to investigate new territory.

The summer before she graduated, Caitlin, a graduate of George Mason University in Virginia, went along with her plans to get a degree in media production and interned at a major American broadcasting network in their newsroom in London, England. She thought it was the ideal placement since she had two semesters left and she would be studying in a field she loved. But then she found out that she didn't really like it that much.

"I found that working in a media setting wasn't for me. Also I had a video editing professor who left a bad taste in my mouth and I think contributed to the loss of my passion for video editing," says Caitlin, who still graduated with the media production degree. After she received her Bachelor's, she took a job at a hotel near Washington, D.C. Not knowing what she wanted to do, she gave it a chance. It ended up not being the job for her either. So she did what many graduates do and took time off. Note that she didn't run right into graduate school, which can be a waste of time and money if not for the right purposes. "I couldn't really think of anything I loved to do and wanted to do, so I got a job at the mall," she recalls. "However during my month off, I found a new passion—baking!—and now I am considering becoming a pastry chef."

For now, Caitlin plans to pursue the chef option. But she knows that not directly applying her degree is okay regardless of what she becomes. After all, her sister got a B.S. in animal science and is now teaching fourth grade, so she knew she was not alone in her decision to stray from her major. "At age 17 or 18 when you go off to college, you can't be expected to know what you want to do for the next 40 or so years. That's why it is so common to change your major or career at least once in your life," she says. Caitlin adds that she has no regrets about not using her degree. Although graduates in the same boat may not feel the same way, she is confident that she'll find something she likes. "I don't think you should force yourself to do something that won't make you happy," she says. "I strongly believe that you should enjoy going into work every morning and giving your 110 percent every day while you really enjoy what you do."

As for her media production degree, she says there is always a chance that she may use it down the road. "There is always that possibility," Caitlin comments. "And who knows? If I become a great pastry chef, I may start my own show and that knowledge would be very useful," Caitlin adds. Her perception is a very open-minded, creative way to look at it—one that's not driven by the overwhelming emotions most of us experience.

Applying Knowledge with Passion

Brenda was the shy girl in the journalism department. A graduate of Ohio's University of Toledo, she felt she would never fit in the fast-paced journalism industry. When a secretarial job came up at a church, she knew she could combine her love of writing and editing and create publications there. "I am an introvert and shy, and journalism is a very competitive, outgoing job," notes Brenda. "I do not plan to go into journalism or work for a newspaper at all. The pace is very hectic, the people are very cynical, and the job has too many hours traveling. I like the 9-to-5 work of being a secretary."

Brenda was employed through a temp agency upon graduation, which introduced her to various secretarial jobs. "I didn't feel I had the drive or ambition to be a great journalist," says Brenda. That was okay with the people closest to her too. She said her friends agreed with her decisions and supported her. She did not receive any guilt trips from them. "Even my college friends that I attended classes with agreed with my decision," recalls Brenda.

Caitlin and Brenda both illustrate stories that might even be considered fairy tales of sort. They show what can happen when someone has great resilience. Both women faced difficult decisions and decided to turn issues that could have otherwise been perceived as negative into positives. But many students have to go through some personal struggles to develop that very same flexibility. It all depends on the person and how detrimental going into your degree field is to you.

When interviewing college graduates, I did not come across many who didn't have reservations about accepting a job that didn't have a college degree requirement, although there are undoubtedly some to whom it doesn't matter. For example, I imagine there is a population of recent graduates who never wanted to get a degree but did it to please their parents, or perhaps they wanted to have a fun couple of years living in a dorm. "A lot of college students attend college because Mom and Dad want them to, and they pursue a field that the parents like;

then they dislike their field," says Dr. Taffy Wagner, a former private career and college counselor and author of *Debt Dilemma*.

Wagner says that another contributing factor to grads not using their degrees is caused by not getting a real-life experience in their field. Many students are not placed in an internship until their final year of college. While her recommendations to return to college or find out what students are interested in by volunteering may not be so practical for students emerging out of school with bills to pay, she does encourage grads to go into a field they enjoy. Perhaps, she says, students can go back to a job similar to one that they really enjoyed in high school while they explore new career options. "At the end of the day it is about being happy and liking what you do," she adds.

I also want to mention those who have a degree but do not strive for a job that requires a college degree are different from those who have a degree but go out of their way to avoid having a "degree-required" job. Most interviewees in this book knew that in obtaining a college degree, they would aspire to get better jobs. Although some are working in gigs that don't require degrees just to get their feet wet, most graduates I interviewed plan on getting the most out of their degrees and moving up the ladder as high as they can get.

Take, for instance, Jennifer, a student taking courses online with University of Maryland. Though she has had plenty of experience as a writer, somehow getting her English degree has been quite the hurdle. So when she enrolled back in school during 2006, she did so determined to get that desired certification.

"I realized I couldn't put it off any longer. I had to have a degree in order to gain advancement. After a lot of arguments, mostly with myself, I enrolled. It's been a lot of hard work, long hours, and days filled with exhaustion. Rather than complaining about all of that though, I'm using it as fuel," says Jennifer, who now resides in Maine. "I know when I earn my Bachelor's degree, I'll be able to land a job as a book editor with a publication house, as an editor for some well-established magazine, or build my business to include more intricate projects. And I know I need my degree to get there. Once I have it, it will open up doors that were otherwise locked, and I will finally have the key to get in."

But as more people realize the importance (and monetary rewards) that come with getting a college education, coupled with more programs encouraging young adults to enter college, is there a place for people who don't have degrees? One report citing U.S. Census figures, states that 37.4 percent of U.S. adults have at least an Associate's degree. Knowing that there will always be a place for jobs that don't require degrees is all well and good. But chances are that because you're reading this, you want a well-paying job that recognizes your hard work in earning a degree. After all, you didn't take all those 8 a.m. classes to flip burgers, did you?

Giving it a 'Go'

Even if you don't want to go into your degree field in the long run, you may want to utilize the fact that you have a degree in general. It can help you get a better-paying job regardless of what field of study you pursued in college. Let's face it . . . time is ticking and you're only a "recent graduate" for so long. There are many companies out there that don't care what you majored in because they see your degree as an example of your discipline and tenacity. So instead of going back to your high-school job or "finding yourself" after you graduate, it may be worthwhile to enter the advanced workforce. You can probably make more money doing so. (And remember, if you don't dig that first or second job, no one says that you can't switch gears after getting some experience.)

"No matter how much you think you don't want to use your degree, there's no time like the present to at least give it a go," says Jean Branan, Director of Career Services at the Art Institute of California-San Diego. "There is a very limited time that you have the status of 'recent graduate.' After six months or so, you're just another person looking for a job."

Branan explains that her institution encourages students and graduates to pursue the field for which they studied. "Many employers specifically hire students for their up-to-date knowledge, fresh outlook and ideas," she says, adding that it is scary for recent graduates to compete for positions against pools of professionals who have been in the workplace longer than they have. But she makes a great point: Many employers want a trainable, blank canvas to add to their company and they find great value in new graduates. So making haste after you graduate to get a corporate job with some form of advancement can really work to your advantage if you let it—you may even find your true calling in it!

Zohar Adner, a career counselor at the Polytechnic University in New York, states that not finding work in a specific degree field is very common. In fact, Adner notes that the lower the student's GPA, the lower the likelihood that the student will work in his or her degree field. "The good news is that there are a lot more job possibilities once you start considering positions that work with your field of choice. If desired, it is later possible to transition into your desired field because of the connections made."

Branan contends that finding a job can be hard, whether you follow your educational specialization or not. "Many students are afraid of failure, not meeting employers' expectations, or are just not sure where to start," she adds. "They have to remember that everyone has to start somewhere and the best way to get into your field is just to go out there and do it. The majority of recent grads will change positions many times before finding that ultimate dream position!"

Dr. Carolyn Kaufman, a psychologist who teaches at Columbus State Community College in Ohio, suggests that The After-College is a great time to try something outside your degree field. It's the period in a recent graduate's life when he or she is probably more willing to start at the bottom with an apprenticeship or entry-level job and work upwards. Kaufman further explains that having life experience and something to show for it—job experience, letters of recommendation, a portfolio, along with a degree of some kind—is more important than having a degree in a particular area. "Interestingly, the piece of paper that says you have a degree seems to be more important than what you majored in," she says.

Kaufman thinks that the percentage of those who directly apply their degrees to their college field of study depends on the major. Philosophy, anthropology, psychology, and sociology, for example, tend to require graduate degrees to work in that field, she says. But English majors, writing majors and the like may need to work in another area until they get themselves off the ground. She commonly interacts with business majors, theater and costume/set designers, education majors, and computer science people who seem to directly apply their degrees more often, "because they get hands-on experience with the type of work they'll do in school and can make better decisions about whether they want to pursue it." There is no one right answer. Apply your degree or don't—you still have plenty of options because you have a degree, no matter what field it is in.

Undecided Grads

While floating through college with my major declared from the start, I was always amazed at the "undecided" students. But upon graduation, I was the one who became undecided as to how to use my degree. At first I thought it was horrible, which is why I experienced so much guilt for not getting a science job right away. Sometimes you just don't know what you want to do with your life—and that's okay. But there are still steps you can take to ensure you have a first job that will build a strong career foundation for you, whether it's in the field of your major or not.

Sean Harvey, a career consultant with Boerum Consulting in New York, states that there are plenty of choices for graduates who aren't sure what they want to do with their lives but want to have a broad platform to build on. "There are many good jobs out there for new grads, but this is a tricky question because so many factors play into what will be a good fit," he notes.

Harvey suggests that graduates who are extroverts with general degrees (in business or liberal arts, for example) may consider something in sales or customer service. He says those jobs are useful introductions into an organization and can provide great exposure for growth in the company down the road. "With these types of jobs, I find it's important for the employee to be able to connect with the product or service as well as the culture of the organization, and more specifically the sales organization," he adds.

Another option is a management training program that provides job rotations in different sections within a company. Such a program gives a multi-faceted sampling of focus areas. You may also want to consider consulting, which is what Harvey did. "Consulting firms have long been a good entry point for intelligent, outgoing, and hard working graduates," he says. Harvey adds that consulting firms encompass a variety of backgrounds for students who want to gain exposure to diverse industries and organizations. They also enable grads to develop transferable skills that can be utilized for future jobs.

Harvey advises students who aren't sure what field they want to enter to use their Bachelor's degree as a springboard. "Given that the market is so competitive and many students experience uncertainty when it comes to how to best use their degrees in their job search, it has become acceptable to pursue jobs that don't directly tie back to the degree. This is especially true for degrees that are more ambiguously connected to particular jobs/careers such as those in the liberal arts," he says. "Students with degrees that are more technical/professional in nature, such as finance, accounting, and IT may experience more anxiety." For students who do know what they want to do, Harvey suggests preparing for the working world as much as possible. This includes visiting the career center, networking and taking at least one internship. You can learn more about Harvey's advice for finding jobs in the next chapter.

As I prepared to write this book, I contacted Harvey for his opinion on "undecided grads" because I realized that there are graduates who don't know what they want to do. I was like this. When I got my first job as a news reporter, I felt confident doing it because I knew I could write. This job was a great jumping off point for me because it also taught me about time management, politics, government and creative writing. It also allowed me to develop good entry-level job skills. I really learned how the world worked as a reporter as I observed multiple industries and people. At the same time, I had friends that had similar entry-level jobs in broad fields and have truly found their calling as well. What's important when it comes to deciding what you want to do is to give yourself the experience you need so you can make that choice. This includes exposing yourself to new industries and opportunities.

Harvey agrees. "I think the critical element for recent grads who aren't sure what to do is to consider jobs that give them a breadth of experiences and exposure to a variety of industries and/or organizations so they can begin to gain a better understanding of how organizations work and the different types of organizations and jobs that are out there, learning where they might fit in their organization now or in the future," he explains. Remember Rebecca from Chapter 3 who questioned the usefulness of college degrees when the people who had them didn't know how to use them? Rebecca felt she was somewhat of a paper pusher at her job and wondered if she might have been able to perform the same job duties had she never obtained a college degree. Perhaps that's true, but suppose that Rebecca might never have known that she wanted to get into marketing (or some other similar field) had she not filed away some brochures and thought about how cool it would be to help clients promote their services. That is just one illustration that shows how you can have a job you don't like, but you can be exposed to other fields within a corporation just by doing that job. A paper manufacturer, for example, doesn't just produce paper. You may work in the mail room and think the whole company stinks. But upstairs there are people working in an array of fields: IT, management, accounting, marketing and human resources. All of these fields may interest you, even though paper manufacturing doesn't. Do you get my point? Use every job as a springboard. Seek out the other options at a company before you scrap it based on an entry-level job there. Most of the time, you will find that if you stick with an entry-level job for a while, you can work your way up to the good stuff.

Thinking Outside the Box

We've all heard the expression to "think outside the box." Roberta Chinsky Matuson, the principal of Human Resource Solutions in Massachusetts, encourages graduates who can't get a job in their career field to do just that: to think of creative ways to cope with—and learn from—the situation. She offers the following tips for graduates who want to use their degree but can't find employment in their field of choice.

- ○ Tune the negative noise out. "If I had a dime for every time someone told me that I would never get a job in HR, I wouldn't have to work today," says Matuson. Be persistent and be prepared to move to another part of the country where more opportunities might exist.

- ○ If you need to, take a job as a temp or wait tables. Having some source of income will provide you with time to pursue your passion.

- ○ Try volunteering your services. Offer to intern one day a week in your chosen field. You'll get the experience and the employer will get an extra set of hands without increasing headcount. Who knows, they may even offer you a full-time job when your internship is over.

It took Whitney a little time to open up her mind to the thought of not teaching English classes with her newly acquired English degree. But when she was graduating with her Bachelor's degree and many of the classmates in her program were completely intent on teaching—and she knew she wasn't—she figured something was off. "I had already applied to credential programs and taken the necessary tests. When I realized that wasn't the job for me, at least for right then, I got a little panicked." See? The blinders didn't come off until she got out of school and put things into perspective. That's okay, that's what The After-College is for. It gives you a few years to live like you're still in college while you figure out what you want to do with the rest of your life.

Whitney remembers that all her friends had jobs. Those who majored in accounting, for example, had jobs lined up at accounting firms. "Here I was, days before my graduation ceremony, without a plan," she recalls. "Out of desperation, I briefly considered a sales job making 80 phone calls a day minimum." Luckily, she was quite the resourceful girl and had the support of her parents and her school's career center to help her select a job. "The counselor talked some sense—and confidence—into me and I applied like crazy. I applied to everything and anything that I was remotely qualified for or interested in. I went to about 20 interviews in three weeks!"

Whitney was hired as a marketing assistant for a mortgage lending company. From that job, she garnered experience, confidence and knowledge, and she has moved on to work for an e-commerce business as a marketing manager. "I love what I do and the ability to be creative keeps me excited about my job," she says.

Although many experts have something to say about graduates who didn't or couldn't use their degrees, you alone can create your true path before it is paved. Even then, you can always create a fork in the road, if you get my point. You must get in touch with your true self and look at what you want to do in the short and long term. Alexandra Levit, who wrote *They Don't Teach Corporate in College: A Twenty-Something's Guide to the Business World,* says the best way to deal with a college degree you don't want to use is to assess yourself and what you can do to utilize what you learned during college, and then apply it to what you *like* to do.

"I find that it's rare that college grads actually *do* use their specific degrees in their first jobs," comments Levit. She says it is nearly impossible for students entering college who are forced to choose a major in a hurry to know what they want to do 10 or 20 years down the road. Her advice? "The best thing you can do is a complete self-assessment while you're still in school or shortly thereafter," she says. "Forget about your major for a minute and make a list of your skills, or the things you do better than most of your friends." Levit further suggests that students reflect on answers to questions like this one: "What type of work would make me want to sit in traffic for hours just for the privilege of showing up?"

"By giving your job search a lot of thought in advance and really trying to understand what you want out of life, you will be able to decide on an immediate path that provides the core skills and experience to take you wherever you want to go in the future," Levit explains, adding that she did her own self-assessment after she graduated Northwestern University in 1998 and started a career in public relations with her psychology degree. "I felt lost, like I had been whisked away on a spaceship and had landed on an alien planet where I had to eat oxygen and breathe vegetables," admits Levit, who says she felt that she got nowhere with each job she took.

Things turned around only after Levit put herself under a microscope and did some self-examining. She looked at the persona she presented to the companies she worked for and worked on overcoming the negativity that was making her miserable . . . and holding her back in her career. "Starting your first job in the business world can be tricky, because it's not a natural fit for graduates who leave school expecting results from a logical combination of education and effort," she explains. "The rules you were taught since kindergarten don't apply, for getting ahead in the business world has little to do with intelligence or exceeding a set of defined expectations."

Levit says that if 20-somethings want to survive making a living in the real world, they have to treat their first jobs like first grade and learn the practical lessons that will help them climb the ladder and establish themselves in their own right. They have to educate themselves on self-promotion, diplomacy, effective one-on-one communication, cooperation, organization and time management. Once she did those things, Levit says she was able to move forward with her life, becoming as successful as she was in school . . . only now, in the working world.

Graduate School is not a Solution to Career Dilemmas

When you're having a tough time finding a job or if you are at a gig that you hate, graduate school can seem like an easy answer to escape it all. After all, you can go back to being a student, which you were probably good at or at least enjoyed. But unless you are pursuing a specific professional degree or need it to advance in your current career, graduate school is often not the solution. If you can't find a job in your major that you enjoy, don't fall into the trap of thinking that a Master's degree will make your search any easier. That will only delay your job search and put you more in debt. Plus, you'll have a specialized degree and there's way more pressure to apply that than there is with an undergraduate degree. Unless you've been turned down from a dream job because you didn't have an advanced degree that was required, getting a graduate degree will only mean you'll spend more time away from facing the real world and accumulate more debt.

It's easy to want to run away when you don't want to or cannot use your degree. Graduate school sounds like the perfect solution, doesn't it? But in some cases, enrolling in graduate school is like crawling into bed and pulling the covers over your face. Unfortunately, you can only hide under the covers so long. Once you add up the costs for school, you may be better off spending a few afternoons in bed to get over the frustration of not using your degree. We'll talk more about graduate school and how to know if it is the right decision in Chapter 5. For now, consider this story that illustrates my point.

Lauren, a graduate of the University of Oklahoma, knows all about going into graduate school. She did it after earning her Bachelor's degree in English education. "The only thing I could think of was grad school—I had no sense of the working world other than retail like Target," she says. "I didn't feel ready to enter the 'real world', and I realized that the world where I was might be what I ended up doing... forever."

But Lauren admits that she's thinking of scrapping the graduate school idea now that she is enrolled. "No one really understands what graduate school is about. Now that I'm thinking about quitting, people act like I make more sense," she adds. Still, she thinks she's done the right thing with her life so far. "I think my major fear has been that whatever I do, I will be stuck doing it forever. I mean, you go to college to learn how to do the thing you'll do forever... but that's just not true. People's jobs change constantly. People do tons of stuff over their life span," she comments. She says that there is a feeling of paralysis upon graduation because of feeling like she has to do what her degree mandates (in this case, teach English).

"But it isn't like that for most people, and it doesn't have to be that way for me. I'm glad I've done some grad school, but I'm trying to focus on what I want to do for the next few years... that's all I have to do." Still, it took at lot of anguish and unhappiness to get to the point where she is now—ready to leave graduate school and pursue something else. At the least, she must find a life outside of school. In Lauren's case, she felt the same frustration as she probably did after finishing her undergraduate degree. Graduate school didn't make it go away. While it may have complicated her situation a little further, it also advanced her education and options. I'm not saying graduate school is a no-no; only that if you go into graduate school, do so because you're certain it's the right choice, or because it is necessary to advance your career.

While having a graduate degree is a requirement in many fields (and a smart choice!), obtaining this degree before you land a job in other fields can also hinder your employment prospects. One of my best friends had to get her Master's in occupational therapy to move up, and she says most jobs in that field require an advanced degree. But my sister didn't need her Master's in Counseling Psychology to be an elementary school teacher. She secured a job teaching first and then earned her graduate degree—and the school system pays her more to compensate for her advanced education! She wants to use her Master's degree later on in life and open a psychology practice—something she won't be able to do without her Master's!

Try to remember that you may not be doing exactly what you want when you are just out of school. Even if you never use your degree directly in the field you studied during your undergraduate years, you can create a successful, enjoyable life for yourself once you get through this tumultuous yet exciting time of your life. Do your best to thwart the critical voice that tells you what you think you should be doing. (I had to learn the hard way to do this—because my critical voice was fierce and persistent!) Earn money to pay off bills and debts for now, and try to have a good time doing it. That's really all you can do. The After-College is just as much a process as it is a period of time. Sometimes you have to know when to let things be. For example, if you're not sure that you should attend graduate school, why not take a year off to work? It won't hurt. Before graduate degrees started becoming a requirement for more fields, most people didn't go back for their graduate degrees until they were in their 30s, 40s and 50s! (Imagine their surprise when they see 22-year-old whippersnappers in their grad school classes!)

Tim Murphy, a consultant at Perkins & Murphy, a college admissions firm, says students shouldn't worry so much about feeling guilty if they don't use their degrees. "People go to college to get smart, if they do it right," he notes. Instead of the fretting, he recommends that students utilize career development to determine what career—rather than a major—is right for them. I have to agree. In my experience, I would have been very unhappy if I had settled into an environmental career. While I'm glad I did some time in that industry, I knew that my true aptitude and passion was in writing. So, yes, I have that silly science degree that makes me a pseudo expert when my friends debate Al Gore's global warming platform. But at the heart of it all, I'm doing what I'm good at, which is also what I love to do. While the degree helped me get my foot in the door (even my first reporting job required a Bachelor's even though it paid just over minimum wage), it was up to me to decide what I wanted to do with my life. For a while I felt very scattered about, jumping from reporting to the environmental job and then back to writing. But I think I had to take that environmental job to make sure I didn't want to go into that field. The entire time before I started my freelance writing company, however, I was using the same skills—writing. So in another respect, I didn't jump fields—just jobs. We'll touch on job-hopping in Chapter 6.

Job-Focused vs. Exploratory Students

You could say that there are two types of students, and how they perceive college influences how they function in the working world. Alex Bitterman, an assistant professor at Rochester Institute of Technology in New York, states that many incoming students are conditioned to believe they should do something that will yield a job or find something of interest. "I'd say that the majority of students that I've encountered in my 10 years of teaching fall squarely into the first camp," explains

Bitterman. He says the "job-focused" student is generally more interested in learning practical, applicable skills. These students, he says, seem to believe that this will give them a competitive edge.

On the other hand, the exploratory students are more adventurous and willing to try something unfamiliar as a job. "I find that these students are generally more satisfied with their collegiate experience, and generally go on to find more satisfying and rewarding careers," he comments. "This isn't to say that the exploratory students have it easier, and in fact, I'd guess that it's actually much more difficult overall; but that type of student seems to thrive on the challenge, and always seems to be happier five or 10 years out than the job-focused students do."

While you may agree or disagree with Bitterman's outlook, he really does sum up the essence of how students evolve into working adults. While some go to school solely to get a job, others go to secure some sort of future. For example, as I began my college career, I viewed college as a vessel to help me get a job. But as time went on and I found that I wasn't interested in academics much—and wound up not going into my degree field—I'd say I turned into more of an exploratory person. Even though I'm focused and settled in my career, I do have more of that exploratory side. There's no right or wrong way to be, but it's an interesting thought process to entertain when you are examining yourself, your perceptions on college and your career goals.

 TIPS >>

8 Steps to Market Yourself in Today's Economy

The process of marketing yourself can be similar to the kind of marketing plan developed for a product or service. Here is an eight-step Personal Marketing Plan Template:

1. **Define your mission and the benefits you offer:** Start with self-knowledge: natural talents (aptitudes), interests, personality and values. Consider what role fits you best: generalist or specialist or a combination. Ask yourself, "What do I have to offer?"

2. **Set your marketing objective:** What exactly do you want to achieve? Be specific, make it measurable, make it realistic, and build in a timeline with deadlines.

3. **Design performance measures:** What will be the observable, objective indicators that show that you are accomplishing or have accomplished your goal?

4. **Gather, analyze, and interpret information about your situation:** Identify your personal strengths and weaknesses: How do you stack up against your competition?

   Identify external opportunities and threats: What trends may affect you and your career positively or negatively?

5. **Identify your target markets:** Who needs to know you, your capabilities, and professional goals? This may mean that you focus your efforts on key managers, mentors or human resources staff solely within your organization, or that you broaden your outreach through membership in professional organizations, depending on your goal.

   Also include the geographic scope of where you want to market yourself, for example, the Chicagoland area? The Midwest? Nationally? Or internationally? You decide what is appropriate for you.

6. **Develop your marketing strategy and activities aimed at your target market:** Take on leadership or committee roles in professional organizations.

7. **Define implementation strategies:** What will you do, when, what resources will you need, and what might be obstacles to overcome?

8. **Periodically evaluate marketing efforts and modify them if needed:** What's working? What do you need to do differently? Do you need to do more, or scale back your efforts?

Courtesy of CareerVision.org

WHAT SHOULD I DO WITH MY LIFE?

By Brett Farmiloe

Brett Farmiloe didn't rely on textbooks or a career center to help him determine what he wanted to do with his life—he took matters into his own hands...along with a steering wheel!

Half of the American work force is satisfied with their job, while the other half dreads reporting to a job they hate, working for a boss they can't stand. As a senior at the University of Arizona, I was determined to join the group passionate about their work. But the biggest obstacle that stood in my way was that I did not know how to get to where I wanted to be, or for that matter, what I should do with my life.

"What should I do with my life" is a question on the minds of many students and young professionals because it's a damn good question. You just spent four, five, six years in school and now you're expected to answer it. You have parents pressuring you, friends and colleagues off to undoubtedly successful starts to long careers—and then you have your situation.

I'm here to tell you not to worry. Not everyone has their life figured out at our age. In fact, no one really has it figured out.

Last summer I ventured on a cross country road trip to interview successful people who love their careers. I wanted to talk with these extraordinary individuals about the path that they pursued so I could develop an idea of which path I should follow. The single most important thing that I took away from 75 interviews and 3 months of grassroots road trip travel was that at 22 years old, I didn't have to figure it out.

One of my interviews was with University of Arizona head basketball coach Lute Olson. At 21, he was pumping gas and cleaning grease bays in a job that required him to work the graveyard shift so he could pursue his love for education. Another was with Barry Moltz, who a week before college graduation did not have a job, accepted a position with IBM because he didn't have anything to do the following Monday, and nine years later transitioned out of the corporate world to enjoy a successful career in entrepreneurship. There were also 73 other people I talked with that all shared the common characteristic of not having life completely solved at our age. That in itself was comforting beyond belief.

The point is that life takes too many twists and turns to decide right now what you want to do forever. It's just not possible. The only thing we can do is accept that fact, and have a determination to one day join the "better" half of the workforce by listening to what our heart is telling us, not what your head, teachers, parents, and friends are leading you to believe.

It's about figuring yourself out first, and then progressively working your way to pursuing your passion once you have a direction and a drive.

Want to find out about Brett's tour and see what he's up to? Visit www.pursuethepassion.com.

GAINING PERSPECTIVE ON YOUR PURPOSE

Paula Kosin, a licensed clinical professional counselor and marketing manager of Career Vision (www.careervision.org), a career planning organization based in Illinois, says that students simply need to gain perspective to find their purpose when they choose not to go into their degree field.

The Power of Career Assessments

"Instead of bouncing around jobs like a ball in a pinball machine, a student who doesn't want to use their degree is best served by taking a time out to participate in a comprehensive career assessment," says Kosin. The assessment includes interests, values, personality, and most critically, an aptitude assessment, which identifies the talents a student is "hard-wired" to do best.

A credentialed career consultant can interpret the results and make career recommendations that are the best fit for the student, and where they have the best probability of success and happiness.

Assisted Job Hunting

For students who can't find a job in their degree field, Kosin recommends talking over their situation with a career consultant who can help them identify why they cannot secure employment. Maybe there are things they are—or aren't—doing that are hindering their job prospects.

"The last thing you want to do is ditch an interest area or career direction without talking to someone who can help you see a bigger picture and other possibilities. You need to do your own work (job search), but you don't need to do it alone," says Kosin. "Alone, it's discouraging."

CHAPTER 5
Graduate School

"Do I really need another degree? Wasn't one enough?"

Even though most recent grads are excited to break free from college, many of them secretly like the idea of staying in school. I mean, if I could have lapped up a few more years in the college bubble, I would have enrolled in graduate school. It's a great way to accumulate more education and accolades, avoid paying off student loans and gain a few more years to figure out what you *really* want to do. But like I said earlier, getting your Master's degree doesn't guarantee that you'll find a career you love. You'll be better served attending graduate school when you know for sure what field you want to enter. With more people our age going to get specialized degrees sooner instead of later, however, it's normal to wonder if you need to do the same.

While some grads enroll to hide from The After-College, others truly want to partake in what graduate school has to offer. As more people get Bachelor's degrees, having an advanced-level degree is appealing for a myriad of careers. Graduate school gives students the ability, in many cases, to get a job in their career fields and start earning money while furthering their education at the same time. Because many graduate students don't live on campus (though many do crash at home with the rents) it gives them the chance to live independently in an adult setting that goes beyond what dorms could offer. We're talking real apartments for many graduate students—a huge plus for many.

Even though I've always wondered what it would be like to get a graduate degree—and have even explored some Master's programs—I have yet to believe that graduate school is for me, mostly because of the fact that I don't *need* a graduate degree to succeed in my field. (Heck, I don't need the science degree I have either, but having a college degree in general has sure helped me move into my dream career.) On the other side, I have plenty of friends that obtained Master's degrees, and most of them needed to further their education to move up in their respective fields. I am very careful to stress however that people should only be there if they need a graduate degree in order to excel in their careers, or if they want to further their education. One thing that I don't recommend is entering graduate school because you're not sure what you want to do in your life. Think about it: If one degree hasn't helped you figure out what you want to do, is another one that's highly specialized—and even more pricey—going to work magic? Probably not.

But I want to emphasize that for many people graduate school was the right choice. Unfortunately for some, going to graduate school to kill time, hide from the real world or defer student loan payments wound up being a big mistake. You'll have to make a choice whether graduate school is right for you. The good news is that you're in no rush at this point in the game, and certainly, there are plenty of resources to help. But here are a wide variety of scenarios to help you make your decision by seeing what others have—and haven't—done.

Graduate School for All the Wrong Reasons

I don't have any secret vendetta against graduate school. I've just seen too many people enroll because they didn't know what else to do with their lives, or because they *thought* they needed an advanced degree. You remember Lauren, the University of Oklahoma graduate with an

English education degree that I mentioned earlier. Lauren entered graduate school to study humanities but realized later that she did it for the wrong reasons. "I wanted to avoid work. I wanted to go to grad school and continue the student life and the life of the mind," Lauren states. After graduating with her Bachelor's degree, she started an internship teaching at a high school. Being an English education major, it seemed like a wise choice at the time. Unfortunately, she was disgusted with the job and began to panic about what she should do with her career. "I hated it so much," she says of her internship. Lauren admits that the only thing she could think to do was attend graduate school, believing her only other option was to get a minimum-wage-level job. This is a very common thought process during The After-College, which is why it is so imperative to assess whether you actually *need* a graduate degree or you are just leaning in that direction for lack of a better choice.

Lauren says she does enjoy teaching and would like to do it in some capacity but admits she hates the hours and time commitment associated with the job. She is also afraid that the job she takes after college is the job—or field—she is stuck in forever. Again, this is a similar mindset to the one I had upon graduation. No one said it was okay to not go into that field. For those students who are the first in our families to attend school, there's even more pressure to directly apply that undergraduate degree. (Hopefully after reading the last chapter, you've opened up your thinking a little and taken on a new way of perceiving things.) Now Lauren says she realizes that college is only a starting point for a career. Your major doesn't define what you'll do with your life unless you let it.

Lauren believes a lot of her paralysis and fear in joining the "real world" has been because she thought she was stuck in a single career. While she doesn't regret attending graduate school, she has been anguished and unhappy at the prospect of leaving academia. In fact, Lauren has considered not completing her Master's degree right now. "Everything I thought I wanted to do seems wrong now . . . I feel like everything I've been working towards might be wrong, and I'm closing doors to opportunities I didn't know I was even interested in." Admitting that she has been depressed since she began graduate school, Lauren says she believes she's going through a quarterlife crisis. We'll learn more about this in Chapter 10. My point to illustrate here is that unless you're sure you want to enter graduate school, or that you need a specialized degree to exist in—or advance—your career, it may be wise to hold off. An undergraduate degree is not a set-in-stone career marker, but a Master's degree is more specialized and focused, and the goal of graduate study is to give you concentrated information necessary to specialize in a career when you're sure what you want that career to be. It's not to say you can't go into another field after getting a graduate degree, but I believe there is more pressure to enter the field in which you invest graduate studies.

Erika, a University of Michigan at Ann Arbor graduate, is attending graduate school and confides that it has put her into some sort of reverse quarterlife crisis. "I got used to things being undecided, up in the air, capable of going anywhere. At the start of a doctoral program, the next six or seven years of your life are planned out for you, and while it's an incredible opportunity for me to be in the program that I'm in, I also feel very confined by it in ways I didn't anticipate." I think the important thing is that her feelings are legitimate. Hopefully she's assessed her situation and is convinced that going for more education is what she really wants to do. Remember, just because she's experiencing some doubts doesn't mean it's the wrong step. But each of us hopefully knows what we want and what we don't. If we change our minds, that's okay too. We can chalk it up to being in our tumultuous 20s.

Difficulties Getting a Job

Bottom line, here's why I'm super cautious about getting a Master's degree and urge people to determine if they really need the degree: *Students who obtain Master's degrees can have the same issues as undergrads face when it comes to getting a job.* I can imagine that having one degree and not being able to get a job in the field is hard—but two? That must be even more frustrating.

I've seen, first hand, a number of my friends acquire graduate degrees. Most of them have either had issues getting jobs, or they have found that the degree didn't make much difference in advancing their careers. While a Master's degree (and higher degrees in general) can be of great value, I wanted to highlight one story to show you that earning a Master's isn't a cure-all.

Mahnaz is one of my friends from Circle K. We went to separate schools for our undergraduate education but met during statewide events. Mahnaz is a Montclair State University New Jersey graduate, and I am very proud of her hard work to earn her Master's in Education. As her friend, it's been hard to watch her struggle, as she hasn't been able to get a full-time teaching job. "I decided to go back to school because I wanted to work with children and I needed a degree to be able to do that. So I went back to school and I substituted during the day to make some money and hopefully get my foot in the door," says Mahnaz. If you ask me, she did everything correctly to secure a teaching job, which can be extremely complicated here in New Jersey, but things haven't turned out as planned for her. "I was unable to find a job teaching," says Mahnaz, who works in retail to make ends meet. "It's difficult when you know you want to be a teacher and you cannot get hired. You can only substitute for so long," she adds. While she's still substituting and working in retail, she is also considering other business ventures.

What amazes me about Mahnaz is her versatility and positive attitude despite disappointing circumstances. Even though I'm sure she will accept a teaching job if the right opportunity comes around, she continues to explore other ways to use her degrees. She attributes her strength to having a strong support system, as is obvious from her close-knit immediate family and her supportive husband...and of course her ever-so-cool friend who is an author.

The Good in Grad School

Up until now, I've shed a somewhat negative light on the concept of going to grad school. So let's keep it balanced and get positive, because there are many instances where graduate school is the very thing that can propel a person to succeed and enjoy his or her life! Sara, a graduate of Kean State University in New Jersey, is one of those people that benefited from graduate studies. She decided to attend graduate school to become a librarian. Getting a Master's is not necessary to work in a library, but it is a must-have to actually be a librarian. For her, she says continuing straight from her undergraduate studies into graduate studies was a smart choice. "I knew that if I waited, I would never want to go back to school and get a degree," confides Sara. She seems to have handled graduate school with ease, and she even got an assistantship to pay for all but one of her graduate classes. "My parents didn't help financially at all, and I'm glad. I liked being able to do this on my own," she adds. I found that listening to what Sara had to say was refreshing. It was great to hear from someone who was able to benefit from graduate school and not have to accrue the financial burden of it. In other words, for Sara, it was the right choice because she was practical about it—an After-College success story. "I think that if you're committed to continuing your schooling and need a higher degree to get the job you ultimately want to have, then you should go to graduate school. If you just don't know what the heck you want to do with your life after undergrad and think that more school will solve it, then that's not a good reason to go on to grad school," Sara concludes.

Carrie had worked for four years after getting her undergraduate degree from Morehead State University. She had to wait over a year to be accepted to a graduate program that she wanted, and that was after applying to at least eight schools. "These programs are very difficult to get into it, especially because they only accept on average 10 to 15 students each year out of hundreds of applicants," she recalls. But getting into graduate school was bittersweet for Carrie. "I received my acceptance letter to graduate school the day after my husband left me with the announcement that he was moving out of the country and wanted a divorce. I was heartbroken, lost and in need of something to grasp hold of. That letter—that graduate program—was it," she says. It's important to note that Carrie did want a graduate degree, and she did not pursue it simply because her husband left her. "Not only was it the one thing I'd wanted to do for years, but it was the vehicle for change," Carrie adds.

Vehicle it was. For Carrie, getting her graduate degree from George Mason University in Virginia wasn't about advancing her career, though

I'm sure that was a plus. It was more about doing something for herself and sticking up for herself when others questioned her actions. Just like Sara's experience, Carrie benefited from graduate school. This wasn't measured by money or getting a better job per se, but it was beneficial because she enjoyed it and she completed her course of study knowing how to apply her education. She also followed her heart and got something she wanted—I don't think that can ever be wrong.

For Carrie, it wasn't necessary to get an MFA in Poetry to advance her already flourishing career, but she knew she wanted to do it. "I knew that my passion was writing (specifically poetry) and I knew I'd get the most satisfaction from pursuing that. I got a lot of grief and teasing from friends, strangers, and family about choosing a graduate degree that wouldn't necessarily enhance my professional career," recalls Carrie. "With a degree like poetry, you get a lot of reaction like, 'What are you going to do with that?' and 'Can you make a lot of money in that field?'" Carrie says she responded to inquiries like that by telling people that she's not getting the degree for her career; and the degree is more personal than professional. "That usually stumped them into silence. But it was the truth. It was a degree about furthering me and my passion . . . my talent. That degree quickly became my purpose, my new mate, my agony," she states. "It was the best decision I've ever made."

Carrie now works as a National Advertising Director for a large nonprofit organization. While she's on the same path she was before grad school, another perk came out of her specialized education. "One thing that has since been added to my career since going to grad school is that I started my own writing and editing firm, Addington Writers, LLC. Additionally, I have received poetry publications and advanced my knowledge and creativity," she says. "All the way around, it was a necessary and beneficial experience."

I highlighted Carrie because I wanted to show that just because you don't need a degree doesn't make it wrong to get a graduate degree. Most students want to apply their degrees, but not doing so doesn't make you wrong for getting one. By all means, if you have the financial ability to attend school and you want to, I say go for it. There aren't many rights or wrongs when it comes to graduate school (or any facets of The After-College, for that matter). It's your life. I firmly believe in experiencing things whether they turn out to be good or bad—life is all about growing and the best time to test the waters is in your 20s!

Swooping Directly into the Graduate Nest

While she was in graduate school, Carrie remembers many of the students being fresh out of undergraduate college. "I personally think it's better to wait until you've had some real-life experience. It contributes to your graduate experience, and bringing real-world experience to the degree always helps," she says, adding that experiencing The After-College prepared her more for graduate school than her undergrad studies did.

Ashley believes that going straight into graduate school was the right choice for her. She graduated from Ohio State University with her Bachelor's degree in Criminology and Sociology and attended the University of Cincinnati for her Master's degree. "In my field, a Master's degree will get you into jobs without having relevant experience (it substitutes for two to three years of job-related experience) and it moves you up pay grades faster," she explains. Ashley says she also decided to go for her Master's because she wanted to obtain it as a personal accomplishment. "If it's something that you want, you should do it before you regret not taking the opportunity when you had it."

I agree. But I also want to note here that there can be reverse benefits—as in real *disadvantages*—to getting a degree. For instance, my sister might not have received her teaching job had she already earned her Master's degree when she first applied. Some companies know they have to pay more for advanced degrees and won't hire people because of them. This isn't to deter you at all from getting a degree if you know it is what you want and need. I just wanted to point out a possible disadvantage, so that you take that into consideration as well. Also, having a Master's degree doesn't mean you automatically get a pay raise. Be sure to research your field to find out if you need that graduate degree.

Ashley suggests that entering graduate school right after undergraduate education is best. "If you go then, chances are, you can still defer your student loan payments and you will still be on your parent's health insurance," she says. Ashley also encourages going straight into graduate school so students remember how to do things like math and use software applications such as PowerPoint and Excel, and she notes that "adult students" are segregated in her experience. "It is just a matter of what you want graduate school to be for you and how your personal life fits into another year or two of the most demanding schoolwork you've ever had," she adds.

Ashley used loans to fund her graduate education but points out that many students in her program aren't paying out-of-pocket tuition expenses. With opportunities to be a teaching, research or graduate assistant, many schools offer stipends that cover the costs of education. Of course Ashley incurred other expenses, such as rent and bills, so she had to work part-time and use loans to live. "This is pretty common for most graduate students though," she says. At the time of this publication, Ashley was working as a full-time temporary research assistant for the Criminal Justice Research Center at University of Cincinnati and looking to secure a permanent position.

Jessica jumped right into the hunt for a graduate program after getting her Bachelor's degree from SUNY Fredonia in New York. She started a job as a publicist soon after and decided to attend The New School online. Jessica is working toward a Master's degree in Media Studies. "I knew I would only be going part-time and wanted to get the ball rolling as soon as possible. I feel the pressure for Generation Y'ers to have an advanced degree is a lot stronger than previous generations, and I am eager to move up the ladder professionally," notes Jessica. "Also, it's easy to say you're planning to go back to school, but as responsibilities creep in—relationships, kids, mortgages—it becomes tougher and tougher to commit."

Going for her Master's has helped Jessica further her developing career. She already received a certification (part of the degree program) and got a salary boost at her current job. "They were very impressed," she says. And Jessica doesn't feel tied down to stay in one specialty because of the graduate degree's broad nature. "Whether I choose to stay in public relations or someday find myself working in the media, the degree in Media Studies combined with the certification in Media Management will give me the opportunity to sample many different facets of the communication field. I will also have the needed management skills to adapt in a leadership role."

Another plus to graduate school? Deferred loan payments! Even though Jessica has residual debt from her undergraduate loans, she has been able to defer payments because she is back in school. She's still making payments on the undergraduate loans and hopes to consolidate all of her loans once she gets her Master's. While deferred payments are great, they are not the reason to attend graduate school. But it *is* certainly a great perk!

Kristen says she wanted to pursue her Master's degree in order to fast-track her career but she didn't do it immediately following her undergraduate years. She waited two years after graduating from University of Mary Washington in Virginia and regrets it. "I wish I'd gone straight through. It was really hard to get back into the swing of school after being away for so long," she states. "I can't imagine what it would have been like for the people in my class who had been out of school for 30 years."

Kristen is now enrolled in George Washington University's graduate program in Publishing. She knows it's not mandatory as a freelance writer/editor to have her Master's, but she believes that it helps, "especially since I'm young and don't have 20 years of experience behind me," Kristen explains. "I look at it as fast-tracking my career because I'm getting the equivalent of several years of experience in less than half the time it would have taken me to do it without the degree."

While her undergraduate education prepared Kristen for graduate school, there were some unexpected surprises. "No way was I prepared for how hard it would be to go back or how tired I'd be after working all day and then going to school and/or doing homework pretty much every night," she says. "I definitely wish I'd gone straight through."

The Joy and Pain of Graduate School

My brother-in-law received much-deserved accolades when he graduated with his Master's degree—it was a huge feat and the entire family was extremely proud of him. After all, in Ryan's career you pretty much have to have a specialized degree to advance. He took a year off after getting his Bachelor's to ensure he wanted to continue in psychology. "When I was satisfied that I had proved to myself that I could do this job for over the long haul and still be passionate about advocating for others, I decided to apply to graduate schools," recalls Ryan.

The rest is history. Ryan graduated with his Master's and is now working with adolescents as a counselor. With his laid back, approachable demeanor, it was easy to see that he would be a natural at what he does. He revealed, however, that graduate school wasn't so easy for him. Ryan says he put a lot of pressure on himself and struggled at times to make it through.

"I had always felt very secure in who I was as a person and as a student, but beginning graduate school was a frighteningly new experience for me," Ryan recalls. He says the first year of graduate school, in his opinion, is pretty much about weeding out those who don't belong in the program. "I for one, like everyone else, felt like I was the impostor. It didn't matter how smart I was or how well I had done over my academic career, the whole idea of graduate school seemed daunting."

Ryan says he believes he focused too hard on the notion that his actions in graduate school would truly affect the rest of his life. His girlfriend at the time was also in graduate school, which added to his pressure. Ryan recalls worrying about letting her down and wondering if he could provide for her if he failed. "Things were certainly difficult and pressure-packed, but I was holding my own very nicely. However, the mindset in that first year is that nothing is ever good enough. So you constantly find yourself feeling the desire to push more and more, all the while feeling this sense of impending doom even when you are turning out quality work."

Ryan remembers when everything hit him one night at about 4 a.m. He was working on equations for a project in his Statistics and Research Methods class and couldn't get through one portion though he had worked on it for hours. Anxiety began to slither in. "Thoughts started creeping into my head about how I would fail and how this would be the end of my career, embarrassment would follow, and so on. Suddenly I felt a world of panic. I was sweating, nervous, anxious and frightened all the while thinking that I had finally been exposed," confides Ryan. He went to the bathroom and splashed some cold water into his face, which is when he ran into his mother. "She could hear me up in my room typing feverishly on the computer without results. She stood there and calmly told me—no, ordered me—to bed. I reluctantly agreed, thinking how I should give up anyway because I was a failure," Ryan says.

The next day, Ryan turned in the project and says he was trying to make peace with his fate as a "failure." He went home and began to study for another class when there was a knock at the door. "It was Mom," he recalls. "She had a bag of sunflower seeds in her hand and as she tossed them to me, she said, 'You always study better with these.' In that moment, as she extended that olive branch to me, I knew that I wasn't in this thing alone. I had a support system that cared a great deal for me and it would never abandon me or think poorly of me if I failed at something that I really tried to do."

Later that night, Ryan received his grade on his statistics assignment via email. It was an A-. "Not quite worth having a panic attack over. And it certainly did not expose me as an impostor or wash me out of graduate school," adds Ryan.

The point to Ryan's story, he says, is that if you isolate yourself or put too much pressure on yourself, you won't stand much of a chance in surviving graduate school. So it's good to reach out for help. And if you can't, like in his case, it's nice to know that there are people around you to support you. "My family and friends have made me what I am and have stood by me through everything in life," says Ryan.

Regardless of the reasons one attends graduate school, it's not a piece of cake to get through it. While the academics may be challenging, the issues that people face personally while in school can be extremely difficult to cope with as well. This is especially true for those right out of undergraduate college, because they are facing 20-something issues that those who go out into the working world face—with school on top of it, plus the pressure to use a highly specialized degree. Graduate school may seem like a shield from the real world, but it can produce the same anxieties that those working 9-to-5 jobs have to deal with. That said, attending graduate school can also prepare you for an even better career, which somehow makes all the trials worth it.

CHAPTER 6

The Job Chase

"Can you take a look at my resume?"

As I said in Chapter 4, your first job is *just* a job. But whether it is your first or your fifth, choosing a gig that you like is vital not only for your career advancement, but for your personal satisfaction. For many of us, work is livelihood. You most likely went to college to have a fulfilling career. While that first job or few jobs out of school may not be groundbreaking—or doing what you intend to do in the grand scheme (it rarely ever is)—choosing a job that stimulates you mentally is enjoyable and pays well is still important. That's why we'll hear from recent grads in this chapter about how they moved up the employment ladder and faced challenges along the way. Some are disgusted with their jobs; some are ecstatic with their flourishing careers. Regardless, you'll gain some insight into how to choose which job is right for you.

Let me start off by saying that the world is your oyster—as in, there are plenty of opportunities out there for you. I know it's corny, but it's true. The U.S. Bureau of Labor Statistics (BLS) estimates that between

2004 and 2014, there will be about 55 million job openings to be filled by workers who are new to their occupation. Although approximately 25 million are expected to be filled by workers who have a high school diploma or less, about 15 million spots are allotted for workers who have a Bachelor's degree. Another 15 million openings will go to people who have some college education or an Associate's degree. So you've got options. Because you can go into any field—not just the one you studied—there are even more prospects. The hard part is finding them and then narrowing them down.

There's a Monster Out There . . . So How Do I Find a Job?

Good question! First off, let me say that we are a very lucky generation to have the Internet at our disposal. Even if you don't own a computer, there are public-use Internet facilities and career centers to help you start off the search. So why not begin with online job boards like Tonie did. This Northwestern University alumni studied cooperative education and spent every other semester interning at a job related to her major, journalism. She says work-based education was key to helping her figure out what she wanted to do. "Now I have my dream job," comments Tonie, who is an account coordinator for a public relations firm.

Tonie began by using online resources such as Monster.com, Craigslist.com and Google.com. She also visited corporate websites that she was interested in, exploring their human resources and career pages. The only site that wasn't useful, she says, was the career page set up by her school. "[It] was created for graduates, but all the jobs were for internships and most of the companies were large conglomerates looking for low-level paper pushers."

But for Casey, a 2005 graduate of Southern Methodist University in Texas, her college career office was instrumental in helping her find a job after she graduated. Casey benefited from emails that were sent through her department, and the career center put her in touch with valuable contacts. They also helped her hone her job-getting skills. The counselors offered a resume-writing class and also showed her how to use the employment database. She says her professors were also helpful after she expressed interest in finding a job. "Try every angle you hear about until you succeed," Casey suggests. "I think all things can work if you utilize them to their maximum capability."

Casey knows that finding a decent job can be difficult. She was interning with a public relations firm that promised her a paying job, so she stayed on board with the firm as an employee. Still, she was cautious about the likelihood of being replaced, and she began job hunting. Sure enough, the company hired someone else and asked her back after she took a job at her current placement, a non-profit organization. Casey says she is happy with her decision to leave the job she thought she'd automatically fall into after school. Two lessons you can learn from Casey's tale: 1) You may not want to trust bosses who verbally promise jobs out of college, and 2) you can always go back to school or turn to job-seeker resources for career help.

Meredith looked to her school for assistance during her last semester at St. Olaf College in Minnesota. She contacted the college's career center and explained that she needed the center's resources to help her figure out what she wanted to do with her degree in American Studies. She hoped they would offer some suggestions as to what would be a good fit. She also used online resources but said they were impersonal and did little to help her get a job.

When Meredith graduated, the job-searching process became increasingly frustrating. Thankfully, her dad put her in contact with a former co-worker who did some networking on her behalf. He put her in touch with a St. Olaf College alumnus. "She was kind enough to do what the career center had not [done]; she listened to my interests and pointed me in a direction—an informational interview with the company she worked for. After a successful interview, I had an internship with a potential full-time offer at the end of it."

Shannon too pulled out all the stops when looking for her first job. The University of Alberta graduate used online boards, networking, her career center in Canada and parental support. "After graduation I seemed to take the job position of professional interviewer," she recalls. Okay, so she may have been a pro at interviewing, but is that really a bad thing? Not at all. In fact, it's good to go on interviews if for nothing else than to improve your interviewing skills.

All in all, online job boards seem to be a hit for employers and job seekers. An Internet survey conducted in 2007 by Bullhorn, a Boston-based global software leader, showed that 36 percent of their respondents relied most on CareerBuilder.com, and another 36 percent reported depending on Monster.com to obtain a job. Dice.com came in at 26 percent, while America's Job Bank was a first click for just two percent.

Aside from cyberspace, there are still traditional ways to land a gig, and those can be just as useful, if not better. Emery, who was mentioned in Chapter 3, actually saw a flyer at school that advertised a job she got. Shannon says a friend of hers called companies she was interested in and began the conversation by telling them that she heard they were hiring. "Oddly enough she has landed quite a few jobs this way, even if they weren't posting any positions," Shannon says. I'm not sure if this is the best approach, but it is a good idea to contact companies even if you aren't sure that they are hiring. You simply never know what they are looking for—don't rely solely on those Internet job boards!

Carrie, who graduated from George Mason University with her Master's Degree in Creative Writing and Poetry, used online resources and also utilized a recruiting firm. She went to New York City for about a dozen interviews. "The only thing that panned out was a position as an executive's assistant at Penguin Publishing. I weighed options and chose not to do it. Then I kicked myself afterwards...could've been so *The Devil Wears Prada*," she says. Now working as a self-employed writer/editor creating everything from magazine feature articles to press releases, she is delighted to be doing what she loves. Of course she has never forgotten her first job out of school more than six years ago as a receptionist at a technology firm. "I took it because I thought it's what you did, start small and work your way up. While I learned some valuable lessons, it was mostly a waste of energy." Granted, that job may have been a drain on Carrie's patience, but most college graduates are eager to get something to help pay the bills. In my opinion, getting a just-to-pay-the-bills job out of college isn't impractical—in fact, it's pretty smart. The other option is mooching off your parents, and very few people I interviewed wanted to do that (even though it sounded darn inviting!).

A Nontraditional Path

Ever so often, you hear about how someone found a job through a nontraditional route. While I would not say that Mollie, a graduate of Western Michigan University, did anything completely extraordinary, her out-of-the-box thinking landed her a job that she enjoys. Unlike most recent grads, Mollie didn't slug around on online job boards and wait for something to open up. Sure, she was a regular on sites like CareerBuilder.com and HotJobs.com. She even tried to use contacts at her school. "Nothing was jumping out at me and I could never tell if the job was for real or not," said Mollie, who majored in organizational communications with a minor in management.

Now working at a boutique public relations firm in Chicago, Mollie is proud that she found the job on her own, in her own way. "I knew the city I wanted to live in and the industry I wanted to work in, so I called a few places and set up some times when I could come in to ask some questions and look around," recalls Mollie. "It was not an interview; more like a job shadow. The ones that I visited that I liked, I dropped off my resume." She used something I call the "proactive approach." We'll talk more about this in a bit.

Mollie says that she also read books to help her nail the interviews she landed. She used sample interview questions in the book and read them aloud and rehearsed answers. "My personal book would say not to be late, be overly confident, and make constant eye contact," advises Mollie. "I believe that it [the key to getting a job] is who you know, or how to make yourself stand out."

While she enjoys her job now and believes in switching jobs to improve her career, Mollie says she is happy where she is right now. "Loyalty is key and any employer would see that shining in a person who stayed with a job for a year, rather than switching around every few months. Plus, staying gives you more leverage for raises, promotions, 401 (k), and building great networks."

Mollie seems to have a good head on her shoulders. She was smart about getting a job and realizes she may have to pay her dues for a while. She also knows that she is still young, and this is a great time in her life to make exciting choices. "Being young means not as much responsibility, not as many obligations, and more room for growth vertically and horizontally," she comments. "This is not our parents' generation where you work with a company for 40 years. Things are changing and a new job means new opportunities. Eventually, I will settle down and I will find that job that sticks with *me* for many, many years."

For now, Mollie's doing as most recent grads are—enjoying steady paychecks and benefits and trying to figure out what comes next. While some her age are planning their next move, it's nice to know that others are perfectly happy just living in the moment, enjoying their After-College experience. So check out job websites, newspapers, networking opportunities, job fairs and your school's career resources. You may not land a job you love, but you can find a decent gig.

Reactive Job Hunting vs. The Proactive Approach

Sean Harvey, the career consultant we heard from in the last chapter, says finding a job is all about exploring the hidden job market. "Searching for jobs on the job boards can be one avenue, but this is considered a 'reactive' job search," he comments. What he means is that by just looking at what's opening up at the moment, a grad could be missing out on opportunities that aren't yet available, or aren't yet advertised.

I mentioned nontraditional methods of finding jobs in the last section of this book. This is different from the proactive approach, but the proactive approach is a nontraditional method. For example, suppose that a graduate meets a stranger on a bus who works for the company he's just applied to, and imagine that this person is the hiring manager who later hires him or her after the lively conversation they have on the bus. That would be considered a nontraditional approach. I'd say that person had really good luck too!

The proactive approach centers on targeted job hunting and a willingness to take risks. An example of a proactive approach would be researching companies in your targeted area and field, and sending your resume to them. Sure, you'd scope out the career page on their website to see if they are hiring and you'd check on the major Internet job boards or in the newspaper. You might even go to a career fair where you know this company will be represented. But the proactive job searcher presses on and sends his or her resume whether jobs are posted or not, knowing that some jobs may not always be public knowledge. In other cases, jobs may not have opened up at the time when someone is searching on Monster.com, so the proactive job hunter submits his or her resume anyway—perhaps followed by a phone call or follow-up note. Wouldn't you know that for our eager job hunter, the exact job he wanted opened up the following week? Things like this do happen.

Harvey recommends creating a proactive job search where you are actively trying to find a job rather than waiting for the next employment posting. "This includes assessing, building and leveraging your professional network. Your college is a great starting place. Leveraging the college's relationships with organizations, on-campus job interviewing opportunities, college job boards, and identifying alumni in organizations you want to work for is part of it," he explains. Sean adds that connecting with professional associations, as well as making a list of the key organizations/jobs you want to work for by doing some research on the market, is key to securing a job.

I can wholeheartedly attest to this approach and attribute its use to 90 percent of my business as a freelance writer. Instead of relying on job postings for gigs, I approach the companies I would like to work for instead. I also network but rely mostly on submitting my resume and online portfolio link to companies. Why? Because sometimes they haven't announced what they need, and if you proactively approach them, they may hire you before even putting out a job ad. If nothing else, they'll keep your information on file and that can sometimes pop up at a time that couldn't be more perfect. It can take months for companies to hire, so if they aren't enlisting employees at the time you submit your candidacy package, ask that it be kept on file. (Most hiring managers have no problem doing this and do look to the "slush pile" when a spot does open up as opposed to spending money to run ads.)

"The key to successful job searching is knowing yourself and your specific career objective. If this is still unclear for you, you may inquire at your career services department to help you with this process," Harvey suggests. "Employers today really want to know that you have a clear sense of what you want professionally and how you will help them achieve their goals." Remember that you can still have a professional objective that will benefit a company even if you've just graduated and have no idea what you want to do. How can that be? By focusing on your skill set instead of a particular job.

Ann applied a reactive edge to her job hunt. At first she used Monster.com and other online sources but found they have had their downfalls. "I feel that move resulted in various unsolicited calls from sales companies and that type of thing," she says. So what proactive measure worked for the Capital University Ohio graduate? "The best tactic was probably joining a professional organization and networking. Ultimately, that's how I've secured all of my jobs," explains Ann, who works in the communications department for an Ohio-based university.

Another thing Ann did to practice reactive job hunting was to keep her options open when it came to interviewing—including heading to interviews she didn't necessarily want to go on. "I definitely strengthened my skills the more interviews I took on; in fact, I made it a point to never turn down an interview for that reason," she confides. "I tried to convince myself that there was always an advantage in practicing with more people and, more importantly, *meeting* more people. Although I might not get the job for which I was applying (or it might not be a good fit for me), I realized that you never know what connections the interviewer has. There's a lot to be said for networking."

She's right. Interviews are an opportune time to practice your technique. This includes things aside from your interview answers, such as sitting up straight and maintaining eye contact. If you practice your interview demeanor, you probably won't be as nervous when you finally land that interview you've been waiting for in your dream career!

Evaluating Your Skill Set

I mentioned earlier about leveraging your skill set to find a great job, even when you are not sure what you would like to do. Peg Hendershot, director of Career Vision, a career counseling firm based in Illinois, says that having career direction before students even enter college—and during it, I might add—will help them when they graduate. "Rapidly changing workplaces and increasing numbers of career choices have made career literacy—knowledge of one's abilities and interests, and of the workplace—essential in successfully adapting to today's job market," Hendershot explains. "The earlier individuals understand their unique talents, the sooner they can apply it to make satisfying career choices," she adds.

But if you're not sure what you want to do, you can identify your best the skills—skills like writing, working with customers and organizing data, for example—and then apply them. Hendershot recommends that graduates assess their skill set before considering a new job, or even starting a resume. Then they can apply to jobs that utilize those skills.

When you consider this advice, keep in mind that a job may not be your dream gig, but a job that utilizes your skill strengths will enable you to enjoy your occupation a little more than not. After all, people do tend to enjoy doing things they're good at! For students that aren't sure what they want to do, assessing their skills via the Ball Aptitude Battery test, Hendershot says, will enable students to better learn what they will succeed in. Whether you take a fancy test or not to determine your skill set and aspirations—two things which can certainly differ—it's good to assess what you want to do and examine how you can create an ideal career for yourself.

Making Interviews Count

Once you land that job interview, it's important to sell yourself. Many of the graduates I questioned prepared for interviews by assessing both their strengths and weaknesses and then grilling themselves with sample questions.

Aside from realizing your competencies, you should be able to explain your resume. For some recent grads, jumping from job to job or having periods of no employment can raise a few eyebrows. "I don't think there's a problem with jumping around if it benefits your long-term goals and improves your experience, but jumping around because you have ADD or don't like someone—that's just not helpful to your bottom line," says Carrie.

Shannon says the decision to skip around with your first few jobs is a personal choice. "[It] is dependant on the type of work that you do and what you are looking to get out of it. If you are just looking to test an industry to see if you like it, then a few months should be sufficient; however, if you are looking to get industry experience that you can then transfer to another position you will probably want to stay with a company for at least six months."

When asked how she felt about job-hopping, Ann said that she believed the younger generation would answer differently than older folks. "I don't think you can put a specific timeline on a job," she explains, "especially a first job out of college. I think it depends on the individual, the company, and the circumstances. Unlike our parents' generation, we have to move around to advance in our careers—title-wise and salary-wise. I'm not saying there's not a more permanent situation out there; it's just not as big a deal today for recent graduates to have two or three (or more) jobs by the time they're 30."

Tonie felt that being in your 20s was the best time to take risks and move around to determine what you really want to do. "I can only imagine how hard it is to change jobs at 30 or older. I think that employers will look at a scattered resume and think the person has no dedication or focus," she says.

Shannon agrees. "I feel it is only beneficial to jump around while you are young and if you are in a job position that you are not liking at all," she states. But she knows that job-hopping has a down side for many graduates. "You may be forced to take more entry-level positions, as often this is the way you start with many companies. I believe that it's always going to be in your best interest to try and work for an employer as long as you are comfortable so you can get a decent reference from him or her (provided you are wanting a reference of course)," Shannon adds.

So what should you do if you've got some resume gaps? "I think that as long as you have good reasoning for your decisions and can explain yourself, you should go with your gut...eventually, someone will understand and give you the opportunity to do what you really want," says Tonie.

But Samantha, who was featured in Chapter 4, disagrees. She reviews resumes frequently as a registered paraplanner for a wealth management firm, and she explains that she tosses a resume when she notices frequent job jumps. "I want to see people that have at least one job on their resume where they stayed for preferably three to four years. If they have any other jobs on their resume where they were there for less than a year, they'd better have a really good explanation as to why they left," says Samantha. She recommends that if you start a job and realize it is not for you off the bat, it is best to consider what is working for you and what isn't, and then search for another job based on that. "If you don't think about it and just jump around, you're creating an erratic pattern of inconsistency that will look terrible on your resume and cause potential future employers to not consider you—no matter how perfect you may be for the job." Regardless of why you have holes or discrepancies in your resume, and whether that can hurt you or not, be prepared to explain your actions. Think of it as an interrogation from Judge Judy—that woman wants to know *everything*.

Eloise, a graduate of New England College in New Hampshire, had a rocky start to securing her job. She had worked where she interned her senior year in what was her dream job at the time. Slowly that dream started to fade and Eloise realized "Wow I'm really not happy here." Around the same time, she was let go from the company. "In some strange way, being laid off was exactly what I needed. It pushed me to see what other opportunities were out there and educated me in the type of experience I needed to succeed in the industry that I wanted a career in," Eloise confides.

Luckily, her intern supervisor recommended Eloise for her current position in public relations where she has been for six months. She says she has learned more in her time there than she did at three years at the other company. "I plan on staying here a couple of years," Eloise states. "I want to suck up as much knowledge as I can so that I can move forward in my career goals. Right now, my career goals are simple because I am still learning. I don't want to jump too far ahead of myself; I want to live in what's happening now and take in the new stuff as it comes at me."

Selling Your Resume

Another aspect of promoting yourself is to play up the positives, and again to be able to clarify yourself—even if your major isn't directly related to the job. Remember, there are tons of people vying for that entry-level job too, so you can't just talk about yourself—you've got to convince the interviewer that you're the best candidate in the nicest, most pleasant and confident way possible. I know it's a tall order. For many graduates, interviewing for a job in a field that they didn't study (much more on this in Chapter 4), forced them to prepare to answer the interviewer when asked why they weren't applying for a job in their degree field. While it's not the end of the world to go into another industry, being prepared to talk about it is highly advised. (My resume still raises eyebrows during client meetings when the interviewer sees a page full of writing credentials then notes a degree in environmental science.)

Shannon has had a similar problem. She has struggled to find a job applicable to her major in physical education. Unlike me, she wanted to go into the field of her major. "I was forced to try and look outside what I studied. I tried an office administrative position and hated it so much that I dreaded going to work everyday. Needless to say that job didn't last long. I also started a job in cellular sales but again found I was unmotivated to put forth real effort in it since it wasn't something I was passionate about and I didn't see myself there long term." While she has not had problems securing jobs, Shannon's struggle has been in finding something that she likes. Her current job as a freelance writer indirectly uses some of the knowledge she obtained in college (she writes on health topics), but she would like to find a position related to physical education. Not being in her degree field hasn't held her back from getting jobs, but it has been more of a personal disappointment. At the time of this publication, Shannon said she was not sure that writing was a permanent career choice. She reported deciding to go back to school for another three years to get an education degree so she can teach high school science.

Richard Marquis, an author, speaker and college success expert based in Michigan, says that it is perfectly okay *not* to go into your degree field. "While it is productive to learn from one's past, heaping harsh judgment upon oneself never is. The operative philosophy here is: 'Why not adapt the intellectual skills I gained in earning my degree so that I can realize future success?' It's a matter of attitude," he says.

Marquis notes that the business world rewards results, not excuses. "Students who expand the definition and scope of what it means to 'use' their degree are ready to meet their world head on," he notes. (Remember that whole bit in Chapter 4 about benefiting from your degree even if you don't go into your educational specialization? That's what you want to "sell" or play up, should you be faced with an interviewer who questions your actions in prospecting jobs outside your area of study.) "A degree reflects an attainment of clear, measurable academic objectives and an enduring intellectual transformation within the individual. Regardless of the discipline, it is a mistake to discount the vital place of higher education in our world."

Better Offers: Which Job Should I Pick?

When you get really good at your employment job search, you may find that there are many offers on the table. Yes, this can be gratifying because you will feel in control of a career that you specifically chose, but it also can be rather difficult to make a momentous decision without any "real world" working experience. You should weigh your options and take a risk. In other words, make the choice and remember that you can always get out of a job if it doesn't work. There comes a point in the job search when you must make a decision, realizing that there are no right or wrong answers. Welcome to adulthood—everything involves fuzzy boundaries and areas of gray. They didn't teach you that during your freshman seminar? Don't worry, I missed that one too.

Many graduates I interviewed noted that the corporate environment, location and pay were all deciding factors in selecting their jobs. "Really, pay was very important to me, but I knew better than to accept a job based on pay alone because that rarely makes you happy," says Tonie, a PR account coordinator. "I went with a job that filled my first two requirements first, but with an adequate salary. I was offered jobs that paid $5,000 to $10,000 more than the one I took, but I knew I wouldn't be as happy or learn as much." For Shannon, the number of hours she would have to work was also a consideration, but this did not weigh as heavily as location, pay and what she felt her level of personal satisfaction would be at the job. "With most of the jobs I was applying to, I didn't really see myself there long term so that was not a consideration for me, but I think for others this would be something to be taken into account [if they want to advance within a company or stay a while]," she adds.

The Money Will Come

When finding and choosing a job, it is honestly kind of a crapshoot. No one can tell you if you're making the right decision—you simply need to make one. Selecting a job is part of the learning process and an aspect of The After-College, and it allows you to create a life for yourself that you alone make. So if your first job out of school isn't ideal, do not fret. It may sound easier said than done, but many graduates know that they'll get to their ultimate destination in due time if they're not exactly where they want to be right out of school. It is impractical to think that you will graduate and be in your picture-perfect career, especially because many of our ideal working situations involve more money and higher positions, two things that only come with time.

Kristin Arnold Ruyle, an instructor at the University of South Florida's School of Mass Communication, suggests that students give their first job a chance. "I don't know why so many graduates think they will get out of school and make $50,000 to start," she comments. If you're in an industry you love, Ruyle believes that tenacity is what counts. Although you'll have to give it a few years until you are making good money, she says it *can* happen. In the television industry, for example, there might be 50 people standing in line waiting for an entry-level job who will offer to do it better and cheaper than you can, should they get the chance. So taking that bottom-of-the-totem-pole gig is necessary to get into most careers. Be prepared to start at the bottom. "After five years, the people whose hearts weren't in it are gone. And after five years, students should have moved up the ladder," she concludes.

When the Grass ISN'T Greener

So you follow all the rules—search everywhere for a job, prepare for the interview, draft a stellar resume, and get the job. But what happens when the job is absolutely wretched? Should you quit and risk a gap in your resume or wait until something better comes along?

Even though Susan, a 2005 graduate of Boston University, says she considered becoming a flight attendant at one point, the communications major got her first job out of college as a coordinator for a non-profit performing arts organization. She notes that her school provided little guidance in the art field, and she didn't take advantage of on-campus recruitment. The long hours—especially on weekends and weeknights—with no overtime made the gig a letdown for her. So Susan switched to a second job as a marketing specialist for a non-profit historic preservation organization. "I lasted almost a year and a half at my first company, which isn't bad for a non-profit. Most people say you should stay at least one to two years, but I say if you're miserable, it's better to leave before things get really hairy."

Though Susan makes a little more money at her current job, she says that it is not what she expected. "Everyone on my floor is over 40, so I can't connect with them socially and have to dress more conservatively than at my old job. I found out on my third day that the hours are 9-to-6, not 9-to-5 as they'd told me before I started." What's worst of all? The job involves a lot of graphic design work—and she expected to be doing more writing. "I said in my interview that I'm not a strong designer and now I struggle with the design programs, but there's no one else who knows the programs either." This puts a lot of pressure on Susan, who admits that she may not be cut out to work in the non-profit sector. "It doesn't support the kind of lifestyle I'd like, living in a safe urban area and being able to travel and go out to nice restaurants," she says. In addition, Susan confides that those in higher positions tend to be bitter and burned out.

Susan was in the middle of trying to find a copywriting job at the time of this publication. Still, she says that sometimes she dreams of scrapping it all and working full-time as a freelance writer, but she knows that is not yet feasible. For Susan, being able to find and choose a job that is suited to her wasn't her strongest skill after graduation. Many students experience the same sort of disappointment, and it has nothing to do with their job-hunting or job-selecting skills. Sometimes you need to get into a job and stay with it for a little while, even if it's not what you expect or want. Susan is being smart by trying to move into something she loves while staying at a job she doesn't really desire—she's got bills to pay and knows that in time, she'll find something more ideal.

I remember being in the same situation. Driven to the point of tears most days at my old job before I started my own business, I recall all too well what it is like to job-hop a little and be miserable after finding out that yet another opportunity wasn't "the one." Even though I did find my dream job and am happy every day to be doing it, I don't think graduates should expect to pop out of school and get the job they have always envisioned. Most entry-level jobs don't allow people to get their hands on what they'd like to. But if you stick around a little, you will get there. It takes time to build your skills and determine what you really enjoy. I had to do the same thing as a reporter and as a communications consultant at the environmental company. Both have paid off—I ace getting work for environmental and technical clients because of my experience in the environmental field and I have the skills necessary to pick up magazine article writing on the side. Everything can work for you—it just has to be leveraged correctly. During the time that I worked at the jobs I've mentioned, I didn't hate them but I questioned what I was doing. I think I knew I was great at writing but wanted so intently to use my degree that I convinced myself I couldn't be a writer. I was wrong . . . here I am. You'll get to your happy place too. Just use everything as a growing experience. In the meantime, I wish you happy job hunting and I challenge you to make the best of your entrance into the working world.

TIPS >>

5 Mistakes College Grads Make When Looking for a Job

By Anna Ivey, Admissions and Career Counselor

1. **Parents are too involved.** The so-called Millennials routinely involve their parents in the smallest details of their lives, even after they graduate from college. Recruiters have come to expect heavy parental involvement in the interviewing, recruiting, and negotiation process of recent college grads. Recruiters aren't thrilled about it, but they have adapted to that reality. You'll stand out from the pack as exceptionally mature and professional if you keep your parents' advice entirely behind the scenes; recruiters shouldn't experience any direct involvement by your parents.

2. **MySpace mistakes.** Do not post anything on publicly accessible websites that you wouldn't feel comfortable showing a recruiter. No racy photographs, for example, or rants about a job or professor you hate. Google yourself and see what comes up, because recruiters will see the same results.

3. **Failing to network.** Networking is a powerful tool in landing a good job after graduation. You may think you don't know anyone of consequence, but if you sit down and draw up a list of everyone you know (including your friends' parents and your parents' friends), you'll likely be impressed at how wide your network is. Each one of those people has a network in turn, so even with just two degrees of separation, you are well on your way to building a solid network. Let your network know that you're looking for a job, explain what kinds of roles or industries you're most suited for, and make sure to follow through on any leads.

4. **A simple "thank you."** When people go out of their way for you in helping you with your job search, make sure to thank them. A short email expressing your gratitude and promising to stay in touch is all you need. Most college grads express poor manners in the job search process, and being polite is just one more way to stand out from the crowd.

5. **Bad voicemail greetings.** Ninety percent of voicemail greetings I hear when I'm calling recent college grads make a very poor impression. They sound immature and much too casual. Make sure to give your recruiters your cell phone number (so that they can reach you easily), but remember to change your greeting so that they don't hear, "What's up, this is Greg, leave a message." A better greeting would be: "Hello, you've reached Greg. Please leave me a message." And if the phone rings at a time or in a place that makes it hard to have an important conversation, let the call go to voicemail. Don't talk to a recruiter during, say, a basketball game.

Major Aside:
Landing a Job Unrelated to Your Field

"I firmly believe that you can get a job with any background, as long as you are passionate about the field you want to enter and you are a hard worker with a good attitude," says Lindsey Pollak, author of *Getting from College to Career: 90 Things to Do Before You Join the Real World.* If you want to go into a field that is not related to your major, course work or job experience, Pollak recommends the following:

● **Join a professional association related to the industry you want to join. Become a member and try to serve on a committee where you will meet people.** This will help you to network for a job, learn the terminology of your field and have an industry affiliation listed on your resume.

● **Start reading anything and everything you can about the industry you want to go into. Read the essential trade publications, magazines, e-newsletters and blogs.** Set up Google keyword news alerts for the industry and major companies so you can get all of the latest news.

- **Network, network, network. Talk to people you know (friends, family, neighbors, classmates, professors, etc.) and ask if they know anyone who works in the career field you want to pursue.** Set up informational interviews with any contacts and ask for their advice on how to break into the field—find out if you need to take additional classes, whether you need to get an unpaid internship before you can get a paying job, find out what entry-level jobs are most realistic, find out if the field is really what you want. (Remember, on these meetings you are just asking for information, not a job. And graciously thank anyone who helps you!)

- **Practice telling your story. Know that people (interviewers) will ask why you are pursuing a job in fashion when your degree is in microbiology.** Be prepared to explain, in a positive way, how you came to your decision and why you are sure now that this is the career you want. If possible, find some way to tie your past academic experience with the career you've decided to pursue. For instance, "Yes, I was very committed to microbiology in college and I enjoyed it. I found, however, that I would like a more people-oriented career. I've always enjoyed fashion in my personal life, I've spoken to many people in the field and joined some fashion organizations and I'm excited to pursue this new direction." If you are confident about why you are making a switch, then other people will have confidence in you.

For more on Lindsey Pollak, visit www.GettingfromCollegetoCareer.com.

CHAPTER 7
On the Job

"I get $12 an hour to do . . . what?!?"

One of the biggest facets of The After-College is your professional commencement. Notice I didn't say professional development—when you start out in the working world, you're just trying to figure out what you want to do and get your feet wet, and as Brett Farmiloe said in Chapter 4, no one has it figured out. Even so, you're going to have to get a job. While you're there, you are going to have to work. In this chapter, I've highlighted graduates who are out on the job, working. Some hate their jobs, I won't lie. Some love them. I think that in getting exposed to how other recent graduates handle work, you'll have a better insight into what you want your career to be like. Remember—most of these grads are in their first jobs, and most of those jobs are not their dream careers. Like I said, that comes later. First you've got to work your way up.

For her first job out of college, Colleen says she lucked out. The Millersville University graduate works for a technology-based public relations firm outside of Philadelphia. Although she had to learn a lot about the latest advancements when she first started, she likes what she does. The office has a family-like atmosphere and everyone works well together. But that doesn't mean that there aren't struggles that come with the job. A former waitress, Colleen admits that stepping into a niche job was difficult at first. "The most challenging thing for me about my job is being at the bottom of the totem pole," she comments. "By the time you are a senior in college, you are feeling pretty good about yourself when it comes to seniority. When you graduate from college and get your first job, you have pretty much fallen from the sky down to where you stand."

Colleen explains that at first, it is as if graduates are at the mercy of those around them. "You have to work your bum off to get respect and basically ask a thousand questions so that you know how to do your job and do it well, and at some point, you can stand where they stand." Yep, that's pretty much it. New graduates are starting from scratch in many cases. But even though you may be a bona fide intern, don't let it upset you too much. You'll eventually move into a more ideal position where you can make decisions and get creative with your work. Still, taking your job responsibilities seriously and learning how to navigate a corporation's culture—even at the early stages—is imperative for graduates who want to get ahead. (Yes, even the ones who are just making coffee runs and stuffing envelopes.) These first jobs may be modest, but there are tons of people like you just waiting to get their foot in the door. In other words, be happy you got in at all—it's a start, and nobody gets to the top without starting from the bottom.

Take it from me . . . I know what the bottom feels like. It can be frustrating and sometimes it may cause recent graduates to question what they are doing. But even a boring job can be useful, especially when the money earned can pay bills! But in other cases, you may wind up getting stuck in a first job that promises a leg up but never delivers. Or you may love what you do at work but struggle with professional relationships because getting the job is one thing. Keeping it? Well, that is quite another.

Inter-Office Relationships

Adjusting to the working world is another change that graduates experience once they secure their first gig. In many cases, a company's community environment was a big deciding factor when it came to grads accepting job offers and actually starting work. They found that new employees can be placed in large rooms with cubicles or shared work areas. I remember struggling to stay focused on work in a newsroom full of other crazy 20-somethings at my first job. With so much going on and my supervisor doing the consultations in the newsroom instead of his office, it got hectic. We wound up hearing about everyone's personal and professional business. Many of the reporters gabbed about silly interviewees and current events, and it was easy to get caught up in the rambling. For me, it was a great atmosphere, but it was difficult to try to work hard and prove myself while surrounded by the mayhem.

Alexandra Levit, an author mentioned in Chapter 4, says a social network can help graduates ease into the working world. It is more difficult to meet friends in the "real world" than in school. Starting a first job can be tricky, she explains, because it isn't a natural fit for graduates who leave school expecting results from a logical combination of education and effort. There are different rules in the working world, and your success as an employed adult has little to do with intelligence or exceeding a set of defined expectations. "If 20-somethings want to survive making a living in the real world, they have to treat their first jobs like first grade and learn the practical lessons that will help them climb the ladder and establish themselves in their own right. These new skills include self-promotion, diplomacy, effective one-on-one communication, cooperation, organization and time management," Levit concludes. Making allies at work can be to your advantage. It's true—I could always count on my babbling coworkers when I needed someone to bounce back my ideas (and we had fun after hours too!).

Tonie, mentioned in Chapter 6, has a similar work setting at a PR firm. "My work atmosphere is very social. The majority of the company is in their 20s, and the older employees act the same way. It is very professional and a lot of great work gets done, but everyone really values the personal relationships they have with one another. There are happy hours and company parties that employees can bring friends and fam-ily to. It makes working so much easier because even if the work itself isn't fun, I have fun while I am doing it because of the people around me. Being so young, this is one of the most important things to me in picking a job," she reports. Sounds like she found a gem of a job!

Chances are if you're in a job where your duties are not even a half-notch up from that of an intern, you're probably wondering why I say it is so important to do well at your first job. I mean, really . . . does it matter if you are miserable at your job until you move up the ranks? Yes, actually. Why? Because if you're miserable, it will likely show, and that can really hurt the likelihood of advancement.

Aside from minor office politics, Colleen states her job is never bor-ing—and that's a huge plus. "Even if I don't have a lot to do on cer-tain days, the people I work with help make it more fun," she says. "Sometimes my work can get tedious because I am constantly pitching on the phones to reporters—I have to get up and walk around or say positive things to myself because just as much rejection comes with this job as success!"

I found that it was the people at work who got me through all of my jobs before I went freelance. Being that I wasn't cut out to sit in a cubicle from 9-to-5 each day, it was great to have others around me to liven things up. Even if the job is bottom of the barrel, you can always make it a little more bearable by having good work buddies.

Coexisting with Coworkers

It seems so long ago that I met a coworker after we clocked out to dish about the day's events. As a self-employed writer working solo, my days of attending the annual corporate holiday bash are also over. Personally, I miss having people around me who made my drudging work days a little brighter, but that's just one of the disadvantages of being a free-lancer, and I remember how much I needed them to get through my previous jobs.

Even now, I have to admit that it is nice to have a work buddy. But I also know what it's like to despise other people you work with. Say what you will, but the people you work with can affect your performance and attitude, which is why the topic of coworkers was interesting to me. While compiling this book, many graduates had good and bad things to say about the people they share cubicles with.

Melissa, a graduate of Spring Arbor University in Michigan, works as an associate buyer/planner. While the Organizational Development major isn't close to being in her dream career, her present job does have its perks. Her coworkers, however, aren't included as an advantage. She has found that many of her colleagues view young employees as a threat—almost as if they are people from a different culture. Melissa says that because younger associates grew up with technology at the core of their learning, for example, and that makes younger coworkers sometimes foreign to older personnel. You have to understand that most veterans of the work force view younger people as a danger, no matter how cool they are. Most of them grew up with a work ethic that is much different from those of us who are young," Melissa explains. "I have found that with time, most of the older workers I have encountered have warmed to me. This is after they have come to find out I am serious about my job."

Cathleen, a Fordham University graduate, says that her college fully prepared her to find a job. She is working in New York City, and part of her job is entertaining brokers and attending frequent lunches. While she has become friendly with many clients and coworkers, it was her supervisors that caused drama for her. She had to report to two bosses: one in her office and one at another location. But she didn't cause the rift—it was pre-existing, and she got caught in the middle. "They didn't get along and I eventually ended up caught between them," recalls Cathleen.

In one instance, Cathleen had landed a big account and was supposed to update the external manager. But the internal manager didn't want her telling him yet. "The manager I reported to called me to see if I had heard anything about the account and I was forced to lie," says Cathleen. "I didn't appreciate the position I had been put in so I handled it by starting to cry." Other than that incident, Cathleen enjoys her job and coworkers. "I love the company I work for, they pay me well, I get all sorts of expense account perks and I have the opportunity to see the world. What I do on a day-to-day basis is pretty interesting too," Cathleen concludes.

Romance Under the Fluorescent Lights

In situations where there are several 20-somethings working together, a harmless flirtation over the copier can turn into a water-cooler discussion that quickly turns into a cocktail party invite. It's hard not to think about finding romance at work for many recent graduates, especially when you spend the majority of your time there. Some are in new places trying to make friends and figure dating at work can't hurt. Can it?

Like most answers to questions in this book, the solutions are up to you. After all, you're an adult now and some of those dreaded grown-up decisions you'll have to make will involve your personal life. Colleen says she is not interested in mixing office work with romance. "People I work with think that another coworker and I would make a great couple and they never shy away from telling us right in front of each other—constantly," she admits. "It bothered me at first but now I just laugh it off and give it back to them; that's the best way to handle things, I think, unless it's something really big."

Alexandra Levit, an author featured in Chapter 4, doesn't offer a black-and-white answer regarding whether you should or shouldn't you date, but she does say that you shouldn't date anyone at work unless you are prepared to see the person every day should things not work. Instead, Levit recommends having work friends set you up on dates and interacting with clubs and the online scene where you live. "Get to know people your age in your department and initiate happy hour or lunch outings that are outside the boundaries of your job. Check with human resources to see if your company sponsors activities like sports teams, travel clubs or charity initiatives. Sign up for "extracurriculars" that catch your eye and commit to attend the events. Once you're there, find someone you know and ask him or her to introduce you around," she suggests.

Although I never dated anyone I worked with, I had plenty of friends that did it. Some could handle when things went awry, and some couldn't. Some wound up getting married. While I personally might not endorse dating at work, I think it's bound to happen for many people, considering the amount of hours you'll put in. Coupled with a slower social life, work often opens up a new social arena, and it's common to date friends.

Sometimes other uncomfortable things can happen in the workplace when you're still on the clock, per se, but not *in* the office. For Samantha, whom you read about in Chapter 4, tension was almost unbearable at a company-sponsored trip. She said she watched someone who had been drinking make inappropriate advances toward the company's receptionist while in a hot tub that were "unwelcome, unwanted, and very upsetting to her." Her coworker decided to pretend it never happened, and Samantha respected her decision.

"But going forward, I will also keep an eye out for any of the young, attractive women in my office and make sure they don't ever get into a situation that could get ugly like that," Samantha confides. "On future company trips, I'm going to keep my eyes out and be proactive about helping others avoid situations like that rather than have to be reactive about how to address a situation afterward."

Here's where I have been: in the bathroom, in tears, feeling utterly violated. On several occasions I was harassed in the workplace—not sexually, but I had a few male bosses who thought they could yell at employees and talk down to us. One boss even punched a wall once. I stood for it for so long and then decided to speak up; and I was happy I did, although it really took a lot out of me. I am not a good confronter, so going before my boss to tell him that I wouldn't stand for yelling and pounding walls in the workplace was nerve-wracking. Of course now that I think about it, no one should have to deal with that. At a large company, it is generally easier to deal with harassment because you'll most likely have a human resource department. At smaller companies, you have to be the voice—or take the action—that leads the way.

Loving What You Do

While many recent graduates reported that they did not find a high level of satisfaction with their jobs, some *were* pleased with their careers. Lacey, who graduated from Colorado State University with a degree in

English education, admits that the job can be frustrating at times. But then again, she is doing what she loves, which in many cases, makes up for frustration. Okay, so Lacey doesn't particularly like waking up early to get to work, but she does enjoy her career as a writing instructor at a community college. Though she never thought she'd get the job, or imagined her students would take her seriously or like her as much as they do, Lacey's got it pretty good. She's teaching four sections of a developmental writing class and working 12 hours a week in the college writing center. In addition, she is planning to enter graduate school.

Although some students miss the mark and aren't sure where they're going, stories like Lacey's are inspiring and hopefully will help you see that not everyone who graduates from college is doomed to have an unfulfilling career. "[My job is] exactly what I want to be doing in my life," she concludes.

Samantha says that although she is a right-brained, creative person working in the financial industry, she has learned to be happy using her skill set in a different way. "Because I'm good with words and communication, my boss puts up with my struggle to get numerical issues resolved quickly, as he recognizes that while that's not my forté, I've got truly exceptional skills in other areas that benefit the company." She rarely experiences boredom on the job. "Overall, it's very challenging and stimulating. I feel incredibly blessed to work where I do, to have the type of environment where I'm challenged, where I'm respected, where I'm appreciated, where I have fun with my coworkers, where I can count on my coworkers, and where I have a really good relationship with my boss," Samantha explains.

But part of Samantha's satisfaction with her job stems from a talk she had with her boss where she took time to tell him what she needed to succeed. "I spoke with my boss from the get-go about the fact that I never lasted at a company for more than four years, and I told him that I had never stayed in one position for more than two years," says Samantha, who gets bored after the one-year mark. "I told him that if they want to keep me around, the way to do it is to keep me challenged and keep me intellectually stimulated." That may not be what you should tell your boss, although I see her point in letting him know what her proficient skills are and wanting to use them to stay challenged.

Samantha has been at her current position for more than four years and says that she has no intention of leaving. Even though approaching your boss like she did may not suit most grads—or work in their favor—it is nice to hear about someone who is pleased with their career. "The reason I'm happy is because they challenge me," Samantha adds. "When my boss has a project that needs to be done, he's good about thinking who would enjoy it, who would be challenged by it, etc., so he's constantly keeping me challenged and making sure I'm doing work I enjoy. He listens to me when I tell him I'm not very good at a certain type of task or that I don't enjoy certain work, etc. and has been really good at making sure that if I don't like doing something that someone else on staff enjoys doing, that those types of projects are assigned appropriately."

While your boss may not be anything like Samantha's, it's good to know that people do exist that help even us newbie algae-suckers learn the ropes. Likewise, it's cool to see that Samantha knew her strengths and was able to make them work toward her employer's objectives. (And don't get too jealous of her awesome boss—she realizes that she's got it good!)

The Entrepreneurial Edge

As an entrepreneur, I decided to include a section for college graduates who want to ignite their capitalist spirits upon graduation. So few people actually make it happen (it took me about two years working part-time gigs until I could go completely freelance), that I thought exploring this facet of college graduate jobs would be interesting. While it is highly impractical for the average graduate to step into his or her own business (unless you want to take over your parents' company), there are more 20-something entrepreneurs today than ever before.

Kevin Shane, a Boston-based clothing designer, started Telme Clothing.com while he was working for a real estate developer. He had taken some real estate courses during his time at Boston's Babson

College, where he majored in Entrepreneurial Business. And what an entrepreneur he is—Businessweek.com named him one of the country's top entrepreneurs under the age of 25. His savvy T-shirts have information printed on the outside and inside and offer a whimsical style. But enough about the shirts . . . let's talk about how he rose to the top as an entrepreneur.

This guy had to do his fair share of research to start up his own company. He even traveled up and down the Jersey Shore—a fabulous drive if you ask me, as I live at the shore—to acquire facts that comprise the stories used in his location-focused T's. Sounds like a pretty cool job, right? It is; that's why Shane's story was worth the shout out. He says that the only drawback in owning his own business so far has been working solo most of the time. "I didn't think that working alone would be so tough. I thought it would be easier, but is gets lonely," Shane admits.

You may be thinking that Shane was crazy for venturing into business at such a young age—in many ways he was very bold and the story is awe-inspiring. That's because it is hard to emerge out of school and get a business off the floor, which in many cases involves shelling out dough up front. That part isn't so practical for many graduates. Shane worked in real estate while he strengthened his business on the side, so that helped. That's how many entrepreneurs do it—build business on the side while working a 40-hour workweek. (I told you it wasn't easy!)

I found Megan to be equally as amazing. The University of Idaho alumni wanted a career in graphic and Web design and used sites like CreativeHotlist.com and Monster.com to hunt for jobs. She knew she wanted to work for a design firm specializing in sustainable, socially-conscious design, at a progressive magazine or at a nonprofit whose cause she supported. "I searched online for companies that fit those criteria and contacted them," recalls Megan, who used the proactive approach (remember that from Chapter 6?). Though many of the firms were too small to hire a full-time designer, she began freelancing and eventually got a job with PETA (People for the Ethical Treatment of

Animals) after seeing a Web design position offered. She continued to freelance while working full-time.

I like that Megan worked to secure her future. No matter what happens with a full-time gig, she's got stable work on the side—and a few extra bucks too. This was ideal because she left PETA after nearly two years to travel during the summer with her boyfriend and find a place to settle down. (They're going to travel in a Volkswagen that runs on waste vegetable oil, nonetheless!) Even though she'll have to get a job eventually, she took initiative to further her career so she could take time off, though she'll be freelancing while she's on the road. I'm always impressed with entrepreneurial people—especially young ones!

In addition, Megan initiated putting together a portfolio while she was still in college and took a required class on professional preparation in which she assembled her portfolio, learned how to interview and was instructed on other business basics. Perhaps this gave her an edge over other students (like some we met in Chapter 6) who waited until after graduation day to start preparations for job hunting.

Kristen, a University of Mary Washington Virginia graduate, is living her dream. She's a freelance writer, editor and consultant. While she's got a career most people envy, it didn't come easy. Kristen paid her dues working full time for a medical association as a copy editor and proofreader. On the train ride to and from work, she was also busy building up her freelance business until it was a full-time—yet freelance—profitable endeavor.

"When I first left college, I was working part time at a newspaper, part time at a magazine, and bartending at night. I really wanted to find a more permanent, less disjointed solution that wouldn't leave me exhausted and reeking of cigarette smoke every night, so I started picking up freelance writing and editing jobs here and there on the side," recalls Kristen. She used resources like Craigslist.com, About. com and AboutFreelanceWriting.com to drum up odd jobs. Soon she realized that she loved freelancing because it kept things interesting and meshed well with her schedule. "I didn't have much freelance experience, just what I'd done for friends and colleagues over the years, but I had great training in newspaper and magazine writing and editing and a relevant degree, and I was a quick learner," she says. "That was all it took. I borrowed $400 from a good friend (I worked off the loan as a housekeeper and as-needed personal assistant for her and her fiancé) to purchase a year of web hosting and to buy a boatload of business cards and some advertising, and my business was officially born."

It took Kristen a while to get over her fear of not making enough money. She pursued a job editing full-time, complete with a 100+ mile round-trip commute. But she doesn't regret it. In fact, she says this about that time: "I'm really glad I did it because it was a valuable learning experience that helped me break into a field I probably wouldn't be in otherwise (medical publishing), but I don't think it was truly necessary." Kristen knew it was time to go full-time freelancing when she began turning down enough freelance work that it alone would have been a full-time job. Soon enough, it was.

So what advice might a young entrepreneur offer to other aspiring business-savvy folks? Let's see what Kristen has to say: "I think a lot of recent college grads have it in their heads that they have to go get a "real job" as soon as they have a diploma in hand. They may feel that the next step—the only step—after graduation is to go work for someone else in an office (or, more realistically, a cubicle) somewhere and get started climbing the corporate ladder. That's a *fine* option, but it's not the only one. Schools and students' support systems need to help new grads see that there's more out there than neckties and pantyhose," she explains. "I think that if more students were exposed to alternative employment—including self-employment—earlier in their educational careers, they'd have an easier time finding and pursuing a vocation they're passionate about."

Kristen also grew up with two self-employed parents, which she said helped her take the plunge because she was used to the lifestyle. You might think that not everyone is as lucky to move into self-employment at such a young age. Kristen's not just lucky, though. She worked hard to make it happen and is a shining example that you can too. "Just because you find something you want to do doesn't mean you can go right out and do it tomorrow. There may be training involved, or you may just need to get more experience in your target area. But don't let that stop you. Take advantage of internships or apprenticeships, and shadow people in your ideal job anytime you get the chance," Kristen adds.

Kristen also makes another good point about starting up your business. "I'm a huge supporter of self-employment, especially self-employment in creative fields. There is such a wealth of available work out there and not nearly enough people qualified to do it, which means incredible job security," she says. "The best thing I can recommend for people thinking about pursuing freelancing in particular is to do a lot of research. Read the books in the field, join some professional organizations, attend seminars. Don't be afraid to ask for advice from people who are already living your dream."

Self-Employment Upon Graduation: Is it Practical?

Being an entrepreneur just out of college isn't always sensible. Like Kristen, I had to pay my dues before I took the plunge into self-employment. I also had my husband's job to cover my health insurance when I did. Don't forget that there is the transition period when you first begin to get your self-employment off the ground. Even though Kristen worked a 9-to-5 gig for a while before moving into self-employment, finances were still tough.

"My income stream isn't consistent the same way it would be if I had a 40-hour-a-week office job with a pay check every two weeks. Sometimes I have a lot of money and sometimes I have none, so I'm trying to figure out a way to even that out a little," Kristen comments. "It makes things stressful sometimes, but the longer I'm in business for myself, the better it gets." Kristen says she wishes she could pay off her student loans more quickly and save more money. For now, that's not an option. She's got some looming credit card debt from college that adds to her financial burden.

Another bummer about self-employment? Paying your own taxes. That's right. When you're self-employed, *you* owe the U-S-of-A on tax day. "Because I'm self-employed, I have to save for what my employer would have taken out of my paycheck for taxes *plus* what I would put in my 401(k) *plus* personal savings," notes Kristen. "I decided on 25 percent (15 percent for Uncle Sam and 10 percent for me), but I feel like that's not enough personal savings, so I'll probably increase it at some point."

Of course there are pluses to being self-employed. Working at home, working in your PJs, taking mid-day breaks...these are all things that Kristen and I enjoy as freelance writers. But on the reverse, there are long hours too. Not only must we *do* the work we scrape up, but we have to constantly market ourselves to find more assignments. "I'm trying to work at higher rates so I can reduce my hours. I'd much rather make more at what I'm doing than have to get a second job or just be working all the time," Kristen says. This is another advantage to getting a corporate day job before you get into full-time self-employment. Once you have some experience under your belt, you can charge going rates. People will see that you have the experience and you're worth the money.

As you can see, there are pluses and minuses to being self-employed. My advice is to decide what you really want to do before you jump into self-employment. You have to have a lot of motivation to work long hours doing your job plus accomplishing the slew of other administrative tasks it takes to run a business, such as marketing, accounting and insurance. Getting some real-world experience at a company will give you the exposure you need to decide exactly how you want *your* business to operate when you're ready to go on your own. On the other hand, you may have a good hand of cards and the sense to play them well as Kristen did.

So where do people like Megan, Kristen and Kevin get their drive? Carolyn Martin, who co-authored *Managing Generation Y* and works as a RainmakerThinking researcher, says that Generation Y workers are more compelled to have control over their careers. "There is an entrepreneurial impulse in this generation, probably more so than in previous generations," comments Carolyn. She adds that the reason for this is that Generation Y workers, who were born between 1978 and 1990, were exposed to technology at an early age, growing up online and benefiting from instant information at their fingertips. *Our* fingertips, I may add. I am proud to be a Gen Y'er. Even still, I can tell you that starting your own business is not easy, and—as I said before—you'll most likely need to get at least one job's worth of experience before, or while, you build your mini-empire. But the fact is, it's possible. More so today, than ever. It's nice to know that there are options out there . . . that the sky is the limit and you can soar!

Workin' 9-to-5: What A Way to Zap Ya

One thing can be said for getting that first gig after college—it will most likely be a huge adjustment because you probably won't be used to the exhaustion. That's right; the tiredness associated with the working life is far different than being drained with a hangover after a frat party at school or from cramming for final exams. For many grads, logging long hours (sometimes in excruciatingly boring jobs) can be tiresome. Even just an eight-hour day leaves little for things that used to be your priority; namely, spending time with friends and having fun. No wonder some of us dread life after college!

I had so much time to hang out in the dorm at school and spend time with my pals. I remember some semesters I had classes only four days a week, and I only went to class maybe three or four hours a day, if that. This left me oodles of time to socialize. While I was super involved during college in Circle K, I still found it hard to adjust to the working life, mostly because it seemed to have robbed me of my social life. I'll discuss more about maintaining and creating a social life after college in Chapter 9.

For now, I wanted to mention the fact that working will be a huge transition for you, most likely. Do it 40 hours a week and you'll find that your weekends may fill up quickly. This is because all of your friends will be working too and can only hang out on weekends. Aside from the social side is the physical, and that is evident in many grads who say they get home and relax on the couch or take a nap in the evenings. I recall building up quite a large collection of DVDs while I lived on my own after college. Since I was flying solo and had only basic cable, I relied on coming home to movies to unwind after work.

Two hours later, it was time to go to bed and rise early the next morning to do it all over again. The monotonous cycle was an adjustment as well.

While my job as a reporter was interesting and allowed me to get out of the office throughout the day, I have to admit that it wasn't like I had to be on top of my game all the time—at least not like Leah, the University of New Hampshire graduate mentioned in Chapter 3, who works as a nurse. She has to be alert for nine to 13 hours in a row. "I come in early and get out late and am responsible for so many tasks. It was be very overwhelming and draining," she says.

Her career is no *Grey's Anatomy* episode, either. While she says she received a warm welcome from the associates on the 10th floor of a Boston hospital, the job is very busy and produces a lot of stress. One thing she likes is that it keeps her on her toes. "My job is never boring. If anything, it's over-stimulating at times. I find myself stressed out a lot and trying to find new ways to fit everything in that I need to get done," Leah notes. Luckily, she hasn't had to worry too much about office politics or nasty coworkers. "I've been able to get along well with everyone up to this point. The older coworkers are a great source of knowledge. They are all wonderful teachers and willing to share their knowledge," she comments. So, minus the fact that she's lacking a few Z's, Leah says she's happy although she gets a little run down. "I love my current job because of my coworkers and there is always a new challenge. I never leave work without learning something new. I find it very fulfilling and rewarding to be a part of my workplace," she concludes.

Melissa, the Spring Arbor University graduate whom we heard from in Chapter 3, says that adjusting to the working world was quite a shock for her too. "No longer was I able to enjoy sleeping in every day," she confides. "One day you wake up and find you have to be to work at 7 a.m., but your body is still used to late nights and late mornings. Adjusting to this is difficult; it took me at least six months to get into the routine. I go to bed by midnight and am up by 5:45 a.m." Melissa also works up to 50 hours a week at times, which leaves her with little personal time. Usually her "free time" is spent with friends and family. She struggles even more to find time for herself to exercise, read, practice hobbies—and even sleep. "When I finished school I thought that I would actually have time to have a life. In turn, I no longer have the desire to go out as often as I did then. I usually spend my weekends just relaxing and taking all the 'me' time I can get," she admits.

Another post-college shocker for Melissa? Monotony. She compares herself to the lead character Peter Gibbons (played by actor Ron Livingston) in the movie *Office Space.* "I wake up every week day and live my life the same as the day before. I cannot picture myself living and working like this for the next 40+ years until retirement," she says. It's that boredom that Melissa says brought her to the point of contemplating attending graduate school or engaging in a new career. "Frankly, I am just scared to death of living this monotony for the rest of my life.

Okay, so that *is* a huge fear associated with life after college—that your life will be utterly boring once you start working. And yes, it can be. But if you make time to learn how to balance it all, which takes time and effort, you can thrive and enjoy your life as you work your way up the corporate ladder. (Got a blah job? Make time to travel with friends on the weekends to liven up your week!) With a little effort, you can regain your life outside of work.

CREATING A WINNING RESUME

Because I've done my fair share of resume writing, I thought I'd offer some tips to help you put together your resume. When it comes to this, people have a million different ways to write and design resumes, but these ideas can get you started.

Thinking Objectively
To use an objective or not, that is the question! It's okay as an entry-level individual to say what you want to do. If you're going to use an objective, don't be too vague with something like, "To gain employment with a growing company." Try putting in some of the specific skills that you want to use.

Another idea is to create a profile. "Energetic self-starter with exceptional verbal and written communication skills" really defines your skill set. Then you can go on to dictate an industry you want to enter, but you don't have to. The point is to highlight your skills at this point, especially if your experience is minimal.

"References available upon request."
This isn't used often anymore and is antiquated. It's more so assumed that you've got references if you're applying for a job!

"Responsible for . . ."
Again, another word choice to avoid. I'm sure you had responsibilities and duties at your job, but it's more appealing to highlight them with an action word. Instead of saying that you were "Responsible for answering phones" you could say that you "Spearheaded communication by managing call flow." Sounds much better, doesn't it?

Cum Laude/GPA, etc.
As a recent graduate, it's okay to note your GPA, but it's not necessary. If you have the degree, most employers will leave it at that. As you move up, these details are not as important.

Graphically Speaking
Put away your "hotbabejust18" email username and trade it in for something more professional like your first and last name. Also, Elle Woods may have used the scented paper to get ahead, but I don't recommend it!

For more great tips, visit www.getinterviews.com or www.content.monster.com.

CHAPTER 8
Checking In on Finances

"I filled out that credit card application and all I got was this lousy T-shirt."

Part of The After-College revolves around independence, regardless if you're living at home or out on your own, and a huge aspect of independence is money. No, it's not everything. But it's a close most-of-everything to 20-somethings. You want to earn enough to make it on your own, and you want to pay off the debt that you've most likely acquired. Even though the title of this book references Ramen noodles as a cheap food alternative if you're broke, you can manage the money you do have appropriately so that Ramen is just a side dish.

At just 24, Jennifer had racked up some school debt—$110,000 worth of it. To add to her financial woes, she also had about $15,000 owed in credit card bills. It may sound like a lot of debt—and it is—but for many students who used loans to get through school, it's quite common. Jennifer, who graduated from Ursinus College in Pennsylvania with her Bachelor's degree and from Rowan University in New Jersey with her Master's, was helpful in talking candidly about her expenses. Her story may help you realize you're not alone when it comes to owing debt and managing finances.

While Jennifer works at a decent-paying job at a public relations agency making about $1,600 monthly after taxes, she also owes $1,036 a month in educational government and private loans, not to mention that her credit card bills are about $650. She says that she cannot afford the full amount of her loans each month so she's had to make some adjustments. She lives at home with her aunt, drives a hand-me-down car, and is working to pay off her credit card debt while her parents help with the loans. It's clear that Jennifer doesn't feel like she's getting ahead—who would?

"To me, paying off student loan bills is like running in quicksand. I feel like I will never get an edge and I will never pay them off," she confides. Jennifer says that she wishes she had been better educated on what college actually costs and had known how to select the right kinds of loans—and then find jobs to pay them off. "I had no idea $36,000 to $38,000 per year would equal me paying about $180,000 by the time I complete my payments," she comments.

Sadly, Jennifer is like many graduates who feel that they are fighting a losing battle. "How am I ever going to be able to live on my own, buy a car, have a family and not pinch every penny?" she asks. In addition to not being able to afford her loans and bills, she says her situation produces stress on her parents, whom she says should be retiring and not paying off her loans.

Jennifer's situation isn't all too unusual. Many of us thought that when we graduated, we'd be happy earning a decent wage and living simply, but money is a huge factor in the quality of life after college. Make enough and you'll be able to pay off bills, get ahead and plan for your future. Make too little and you'll probably feel stuck in a rut, believing that you will never be able to get ahead.

Let me say that I've been there. Upon graduation I left Stockton College with approximately $18,000 in loans trailing behind me. More so, I had about $5,000 in credit card debt—and the sad thing was that I couldn't pinpoint where it came from. While my debt was on a smaller scale, it was still very overwhelming, especially since I knew I wanted to continue living on my own, and I knew that was going to be expensive. My mother had done all she could to help me through college and couldn't give much financial assistance anymore. There I was, on my own in more ways than one.

I'll be honest—it took years to get my finances cleaned up (I am *still* paying off the student loans, although the credit card debt has been eradicated). There were nights when I lay in bed worrying about my finances and my future, and I was sick to my stomach. To top it off, the only way I could make decent money at the time was to take jobs that I didn't like so much. There were good aspects to my jobs, but they all paid much less than I had anticipated. I wish I could say that gaining a healthier financial footing was easy, but it's not. It's hard to think about saving for retirement like all the experts do when you have to charge your lunch on a credit card, which I did more times than I'd like to admit.

As you read through this chapter, I recommend that you digest the information and be proactive when it comes to digging out of any debt. If you're lucky not to have debt, then you're a step ahead and can move on to investing and saving. Regardless of your financial situation, I hope the information here helps you make fiscally healthy decisions—because you can, regardless of the financial predicament you're in.

Putting It on the Plastic

Like many recent grads, Marissa found herself independent of her parents' finances once she graduated from Rutgers University in New Jersey. As she moved into law school, she was able to support herself by taking out loans and working part-time. Now working as a lawyer, she's paying off her debt and managing her money well. She even owns her own home and has married.

But Marissa says her credit card balance is a little higher than she would like. Of course going through the wedding process put a strain on her finances, and she wasn't able to pay off the entire amount each month during that time. Now that she is married, she and her spouse are able to pay on her loans by working within a budget. But she knows that many young adults her age aren't able to properly handle money, especially when it comes to credit cards.

"I think young people have credit problems because they don't view the cards as spending their own money. I always viewed it as 'my money' I owed on the cards, and I never liked paying the credit card finance charges," Marissa explains. She says her motto was that if she didn't have enough money in her bank account to cover a purchase, she wouldn't put it on the credit card. Marissa recognizes there are situations that arise in life that make using credit cards a necessity, but recent grads need to make sure they use their credit cards responsibly. "To go into credit card debt over clothes and makeup is ridiculous in my view," she adds.

Although she is financially content for the time being, Marissa admits that she could have saved a lot of money during law school had she lived at home. This simple tactic is what plenty of recent graduates do—though many do so reluctantly. Still, living at home after college can have its benefits. "Don't move out of your parents' home if you can live there," says Marissa. "Save the money you would spend on rent and invest it in a money market account or something relatively safe, but still interest bearing. Save for a down payment on a house so that when you want to move out, you can buy instead of rent."

Eloise, a graduate of New England College in New Hampshire, agrees that money is certainly a struggle after you graduate from school—even when you have a well-paying job. "Between rent, credit card payments, college loans, car insurance, train/subway tickets and food, my bank account has gone into the negatives a couple of times," says Eloise, who lives in Bellmore, New York and works as a public relations coordinator.

Eloise says that she wishes she had more of a financial cushion but admits that she has sacrificed that for life working in the big city. In doing so, she has relied on credit to help her adapt to adult life. While she has not run into an extreme situation involving collections because she pays her bills on time, Eloise says she has problems making a dent in the balance because of the hefty finance charges. During college her parents helped to pay on her debt. When she graduated, they handed over the bill to her—a bill that still had somewhat of a large balance. "I should have played my cards right from the beginning," she laments.

While some students blame vendors on campus for their credit problems, Eloise says she wishes her parents had told her more about money earlier on. "Maybe I wouldn't be in the hole I'm in now!" she adds. Students probably should take some initiative to manage their own finances while they are in school. My mother sat me down to go over my college financing before I even stepped foot on campus. In conversing with her throughout my college years, I learned a lot about good debt, bad debt, and other aspects of finance. If you can, talk to your parents or check out some library books to teach yourself about loans, debt, saving and investing. It's well worth it.

Financial Blunders

I will be the first to admit that my finances were beyond messy after I graduated. I didn't earn much at my first job. But coming out of college with credit card debt was an added pressure that emotionally weighed me down. Many students experience this, and it can really contribute to life after college not being all it was cracked up to be.

Melissa, previously mentioned in Chapter 3, recalls mismanaging her credit in college. She says she's not sure who was to blame for it, but she does think schools should have stricter standards on vendors. "Credit problems? I think that's my middle name to be honest," Melissa says. "I was sucked in by all the credit card offers I received when I hit the big 18. If I needed clothes, books or food, I turned to my credit cards to bail me out when I was short on cash." While she was only in debt about $3,000 at the time of this publication, Melissa confides that she fell behind on payments when she hit some rough spots, and she is now paying back money to the collections agencies. "I'm not sure who to blame for falling into this. Maybe it was my parents. Maybe it was the schools that didn't protect me. Who knows? All I know is that I had a rude awakening when they pulled the credit report because I needed financing for something," Melissa adds. "I think colleges should do more to limit what vendors come and hang out on campus offering free goods to those who apply for credit. It definitely should be limited or even outlawed on campuses."

For now, Melissa's living mostly paycheck to paycheck. "I screwed up badly with credit cards and am still working to pay that off. I will have a lot of it paid off within the next year or so; but until then, I will only be able to enjoy the basics of life," she comments. Melissa does work with a budget now, and she says she uses Microsoft Excel to track her expenses. Although she still has college debt to pay off, she's been trying to hold off on that. "I will be starting my graduate degree and will keep pushing off the repayment of those school loans for as long as I can," Melissa adds. "I am going to try, however, to work on paying off the interest before I have to begin paying off the principal. I just want to try and manage the other bills that I have to get paid off first."

Luckily, Melissa is working full-time and her boss has promised her a bump in pay. "I am hoping that I can be wise enough and account-able enough to put back some of that difference in pay into savings and the rest towards my bills," she says, adding that saving as much as possible is necessary. "Some day your car will break down and you were not smart enough to save money to fix it. I have been there and I do not want to have to beg my parents for money ever again."

Of course it is easy to play the blame game with the rents before and after you graduate. But once you get that degree, you are basi-cally on your own—so your financial situation will depend largely on your skills at money management. These skills need to be developed just like interview skills do. There are many issues that contribute to hardships as a newly working adult. An obvious challenge can be that your first job (or a few jobs) may be entry-level opportunities that pay very little. Another is the desire to blast into adult life without the fiscal resources to do so. Whether you jet into an apartment on your own or finance a new ride that screams "suave young profes-sional," your first financial steps as a working adult, if drastic, can turn into a financial disaster.

Eloise didn't experience a catastrophe, but she was yearning to bust out of her parents house into her own place in Long Island where she commutes to and from Manhattan for work. While she loves the independence, Eloise admits that she flew the coop too quickly. Believe me, I know how it is to yearn to get out of your parents' house, as much as you do love them. Unless you hit the lottery, your best bet is to live with a roommate or live in a refurbished motel on the off season like I did. This will at least get you out of the house—but remember, you'll have to fully make it on your own. Many parents don't offer as much financial support when you move out. Can you blame them?

The Cause of It All

Why do so many young people have financial issues? "When you are in college, you are in a bubble," Eloise explains. "Everything is right there, handed to you, and the responsibility that you have is slim to none. At the time, you think you are ruling the world, and it *should* be as fun as it can be. But as soon as graduation day comes—as soon as that letter comes saying 'Sorry no more health insurance for you'—that's the day you need to wake up and realize you are really on your own." She adds that jumping the gun on starting your "adult" life can contribute to financial setbacks, as it did in her case. Eloise advises students to plan their next steps as carefully as possible. "Realize you are not indestructible, and neither is your bank account!"

While it's sometimes easy for graduates to give advice after they go through difficult situations themselves, Eloise does raise a valid point about being in a protective pocket during college and how much life changes when you're thrust into the working world. She got me to thinking: Can zooming into adult life add to your financial demise? Truthfully, it varies from person to person. Chances are if you're working, you can afford to move out on your own so long as you find an affordable place. While I don't regret moving into the casa de beach motel, I do admit that I blew out of my mother's house a little prematurely. Luckily, I had dirt-cheap rent, which made it possible for me to exist on my own while earning a laughable wage at my first real job. Even though I look back and think about how horrible my post-college debt was, there are some students who have had it worse. To touch on their stories is valuable in that it may show you how important financial management is.

Cap, Gown, Debt

Let's face it, many of us will—or have already—graduated college with a "balance due" figure looming over our heads. Whether you put your school tuition into a loan or on a credit card, coming out of your undergraduate education with this debt is more acceptable than coming out with a credit card racked up from personal expenses and reckless spending. No matter how your financial situation stacks up now, it's never too late to start living a more financially fit life; and if you are in a hole, you *can* get out of it.

Jessica, a graduate of Kean University in New Jersey, graduated college $15,000 in debt. "The majority of the debt was from personal spending . . . trying to keep up with other people who had the latest fashions, eating out and having a new car that I bought with little guidance. I spent money as if I had it," recalls Jessica. The problem for her was that her job during college only paid $20,000 a year, which didn't leave much wiggle room for living expenses on top of paying off the debt she owed. After college, Jessica worked as a lab technician at a small biotech company and says she had to consolidate her loans because she wasn't able to make the minimum payments on her credit debts. "From that point on, I rarely used my credit card because I saw how quickly the amount can snowball. My ability to get a credit card was so easy! I was given a lot of credit! I could have bought a car on that amount." Ha—she did!

Julie-Ann, who graduated from University of Massachusetts at Amherst, also fell prey to the wide array of credit card vendors on campus who offered her spending alternatives (and ridiculous freebies). "I definitely think that the wide availability of cards to students is a problem. We are given too much credit without being taught how to use it properly. I think that they should have required courses in 'managing your life and your money' or something in your first year. It certainly would have helped me!" she asserts.

Sara, who completed her Bachelor's degree at Thiel College in Pennsylvania and got her Master's from Kent State University in Ohio, says students and grads shouldn't blame vendors. She and her husband pay their credit cards in full each month and she says they never charge more than they can afford. "I don't think we should blame credit card companies for debt problems. People have to learn how to use credit cards responsibly and not charge things they can't afford."

Jessica and Julie-Ann both said they wished there had been a class on credit counseling during college. But I have to be honest here: would anyone really take that class? I wouldn't have. At the time, I thought I was in control and was betting on a well-paying job to pay off the debt. I understand the need for prevention, but I doubt most students would take a course or go for financial counseling until after they graduate. The good news is that if and when you are ready for financial help, there are plenty of low-cost—and even *free*—tools to help get you out of the red and back in the green.

While Jessica has moved into a new job as a scientist and makes enough money to cover expenses and also invest, she says financial management is key to getting one's finances together. Now married and a homeowner, she is doing much better economically but still pays attention to her finances. "I have a budget for my household items and bills. A set amount of money is deducted from my husband's and my accounts every month for our mortgage, utilities and other expenses. The remainder of the money goes to individual bills, 401(k)s, Roth IRAs, and other savings." They are finally beginning to get ahead.

So, see? You'll be able to pay off the debt with a lot of hard work and dedication. Assuming you're not spending needlessly, there are plenty of ways to take control of your finances. The good news is that you don't have to eat Ramen forever.

Staying Responsible with Your Green

For Lacey, a Colorado State University graduate now working as a teacher and heading to graduate school, living at home enabled her to reduce expenses and pay her bills. Lacey's parents helped with food and comfort, but the rest was up to her. She relied on a credit card now and then to afford some big-ticket items, most of which were necessities.

Overall, Lacey says credit cards aren't the demise for new grads so long as they are accountable for the debt.

"I think that if people are responsible, they won't find themselves with credit problems," says Lacey. "I think that, in the end, young people need to learn to be responsible for themselves and their money, so having credit vendors on college campuses isn't that big of a problem. If someone's going to be irresponsible and spend more than they have, they'll do that whether credit card vendors tempted them with a T-shirt or not." Lacey uses a budget to stay on track. "I do have a budget, and I have to live on a budget. I don't make that much money, and I have credit card bills to pay off," she concludes.

Kelly, a University of Washington graduate, says she sticks to a budget too. "I cannot live paycheck to paycheck—it would kill me," she confides. Kelly says that the reason so many young adults have financial problems is because of the credit card companies that target young adults while they're in school. The other part of that is there are many students who don't understand how detrimental using credit cards can be. It's easy to blame the vendors but it's not responsible. "I think the market is taking advantage of young people," Kelly continues. "They don't know what they are doing or how they are ruining their futures. There need to be new laws."

Kelly certainly has a point although there may be those who disagree. Still, regardless of whose fault it is that young people can have financial difficulties before filling out their first W-2, it all comes down to being responsible. At this point, you may already have fallen victim to the credit card vendors that most likely lined your campus with free mugs, hats and T-shirts. Even so, college isn't the only time when many of us spend impulsively. It happens to college grads too. Even if you can afford a new pad, for example, you may not be able to pay for all the ritzy new furnishings that you put on your credit card.

Regardless of where you fall on the credit card issue, remember that you can move forward. With a little forethought and planning, you can take control of your financial situation and smartly manage your money from here on out.

Financial Health and Health Insurance

Ashley, an Ohio State University graduate, admits that she almost got into a financial rut when she started using credit cards. "I started heading down the path of putting things on credit cards when I was first away at college, but I realized it wasn't the way to go and stopped that habit," she recalls. While she feels that credit vendors at schools take advantage of students, she points out that the credit offers at malls and other public places are just as bad. "Every store wants to give you a card with an astronomical interest rate. It's not a good way to start life as an adult, that's for sure," she says. Once she realized this, Ashley made it a point to stay away from abusing credit.

Now working, Ashley has a job that covers her expenses, but she shares that she still lives paycheck to paycheck. "It feels like you are in this rut and are never going to make any progress with bills," Ashley admits. She says she works odd jobs so she can always rely on extra cash. For someone who sounds like she's having a hard time, Ashley also sounds really smart when it comes to money, and she seems to be a really hard worker. At least she doesn't have credit problems!

Ashley seems to have a healthy attitude about money that many college graduates in their early 20s might find it wise to emulate. She advises other grads to explore financial matters such as health insurance, since many haven't had to pay for their own before. "Health insurance can be a big shock to recent grads if they don't have a job with benefits. Most of us have been on our parents' plans for five or six years and now we will be responsible for paying it."

Ashley's also very careful about paying off her student loans, and she says students need to be on top of things with their lenders. This includes knowing exactly how much money they owe to each. "Most lenders offer forbearance or deferment if you get behind or need help," Ashley explains. "But if you default, your credit will be damaged for a long time." We'll discuss dealing with your loan lenders later on in this chapter.

Creating a PLAN for Your Financial Future

Is it really possible that you don't have to fall into a financial slump as you emerge into The After-College? Yes! Of course, I must admit, I made some monetary mistakes before and after I graduated. Luckily, I got back on track—and so can you.

That's what Stanley Kershman, the author of *Put Your Debt on a Diet: A Step-by-Step Guide to Financial Fitness* says. Also known as The Debt Doctor, Kershman explains that graduating college marks the beginning of a new life, including a new financial world. "You have a choice: you can let money (or, more specifically, debt) control you, or you can seize control of it, and make it work for you."

Kershman's blueprint for financial success is laid out in what he calls a PLAN:

1. **Prepare.** Gather together all of the paperwork that relates to your financial situation. Put it all in one place and then group it by category (insurance policies, debts, etc.). You need to assess where you are. How much money is coming in, and how much is going out?

2. **Leverage.** You've likely done a lot of learning and research-ing in college: make that work for you now. Use those skills to help you research your financial situation and the elements that should go into your plan. Read books and magazines. Surf the Internet. Talk to a professional. Personal banking representa-tives, non-profit credit counselors, and local community-based experts can be a wealth of knowledge—they may even know of trustworthy programs that can help recent graduates pay down their student loans, wisely choose car loans or mortgages, or launch businesses.

3. **Analyze.** Figure out where your problem areas might be. Where are you having trouble: debt repayments, keeping up with in-surance policy payments, etc.? Identify the issues, and you're halfway to solving them, Kershman adds. Then investigate your

wiggle room. Here's where you're looking for solutions, whether it's searching for another job, reducing discretionary spending, or readjusting your debt load. This can be especially hard for students who are used to their parents' support and no longer have enough to maintain a lifestyle they're used to.

Keep in mind that if you're already in debt, the worst thing you can do is add to your debt load every month. Pay for each item as you go, Kershman says. "Don't rack up your credit card bills even further. If you can't afford it, don't buy it. If it's [truly] an essential item, figure out how to increase your income or decrease other expenses in order to afford it."

4. **Name It.** Decide what you need in your financial plan and what you want in it (your goals), and how you're going to achieve it all. Keep in mind that you need to protect yourself, and your family if you have one. Think about what could happen if you don't have adequate life, health or disability insurance: it's too great a risk to take.

Also think about how much you're currently paying in rent, whether it is to your parents or an outside landlord. Take a look at the local real estate market, and see what you can buy for the equivalent monthly payment. If you need to, get creative—buy a property with a friend or family member (make sure you have a legal agreement in place to protect everyone's interests and to lay out rights and responsibilities). The sooner you start investing in your own future, instead of your landlord's, the better off you'll be. (Owning property just out of college is probably way ahead of where you're thinking in terms of living, and that's okay. It's just good to think about how to position yourself financially, especially if you do want to own a place in a few years.)

Kershman says that putting your plan into writing will help to move it along and make it more of a set-in-stone reality. He advises recent grads to check progress regularly and to reward themselves for good behavior. "Small successes lead to bigger ones," he adds.

Crunchin' Numbers: Creating a Budget

Many of the students I interviewed used a budget to organize their finances. Even when not strictly followed, it still helps you face your finances and plan for the future. Julie-Ann agrees. "I work on a loose budget, planning out the bills I have to pay at the beginning of each month. I am a very organized person in general; but if I didn't keep close track of my money, I would definitely fall short every month. I always have a general idea of what I have left in my bank account so that I know what I can spend when I go out on the weekends." This approach not only helps you limit your spending, but it gives you the opportunity to think through what purchases you can afford.

So, how exactly do you lay out a budget? (Chances are, you didn't learn how to do this during your many years as a student!) Kershman recommends tracking your income and expenses to figure out how much is coming in, how much is going out and what the difference is. If you're already struggling with debt as many students are, you may already be in the hole each month. Kershman suggests assessing what you can do to increase the amount you can repay each month (which will save you plenty of interest charges in the future). Try increasing your income (getting a second job) or decreasing your expenses (trading a daily latte for a regular coffee saves you $520 or more a year).

Personally, I think if you're smart about money as a whole, it doesn't matter whether you use a budget or some other means of tracking your finances. (Budget use really does depend on the individual. I didn't use a budget but I did keep track of my finances.) Of course if you're not sure or feel like you have a tendency to overspend, setting up a budget is the way to go. I probably should have created a budget but found it restricting by nature. Plus, I didn't have the discipline to keep track of every expenditure, but I guess that's another plus for using a budget!

Inexpensive Adventures

Jessica said something that caught my attention. She confided that she had to cut back on spending when it came to her personal expenditures. Still, she said there are little things that we all enjoy and shouldn't have to give up during such a hard time in our lives. Because money isn't the only pressure as a new graduate, you're going to need to take care of yourself even if you are on the "broke" side of your finances.

I remember those days as a recent graduate when I was living paycheck to paycheck, never able to save a dime and always overwhelmed by my bills. I was making the same $20,000 a year that Jessica made as a college student *at my first real job*. I had little money to enjoy myself. I wasn't spending needlessly like I had been in college; I was just trying to survive, living in my refurbished motel room/apartment/independence pad.

While I don't want to encourage you to blow a ton of cash pampering yourself while you're in the midst of financial tightness, I do think it's important to add a bit about taking care of yourself mentally and emotionally while you're working to pay off debt—and even probably very depressed about having it in the first place. In my case, I didn't eat as well as I could have because generally foods that are worse for you are more affordable. (Hello, ramen noodles!) I didn't go out to a lot of dinners or cocktail parties with friends and coworkers, though I do remember splurging on a few things even though I knew it was bad for me financially. Feeling financially "stuck" was extremely crushing. The topic of money always sent me into feelings of hopelessness and panic. While I did my best to create a repayment schedule (like I said, I should have used a budget!) I felt very trapped. I mentally kicked my butt every day, punishing myself for giving in to credit card vendors at school and spending my money on . . . I still don't know exactly what. After all, I had a degree, didn't that mean I was supposed to be successful? And weren't successful people financially free?

At that point, I wasn't free at all. My plan of action included focusing on my career and moving up the ranks until I finally got to a place where I was financially stable and able to save. Oh yeah, and happy. It took a while, but I did get there. In my field, copywriting, most projects pay very well and in tasty lump sums. I steadily started paying off bills—even overpaying them—once I found my true career calling. (Not only was I happy, but I made money to prove it!) I sent payments to "friends" at Visa, MasterCard, and the U.S. Department of Education. Slowly but surely, I chipped away at my debt.

I share my story in hopes that it will inspire you to take care of your checkbook—and yourself. The hardest part about dealing with my financial ickiness was the emotional factor of it all. Seeing "late fee" and "delinquency" written on bills made me want to lie in bed. Even though I got "out" of my financial mess, it was still one of the biggest struggles of my early 20s and probably what motivated me to be a workaholic, which now works to my benefit. Truthfully, I believe you have the power to find an "out." You just have to get strong enough to take control of it all. With financial counseling and information at our fingertips via the Web, you can get the tools you need to take charge. (I've also included a reference area with some great sites and books on financial management in the appendices.)

If you're worried about not being able to afford self-care to cope with the strain of finances and the rest of your After-College stressors, don't be. While you're in a financial rut, there are plenty of inexpensive—even free—things you can do so you don't skimp on nurturing your soul, which is so important when you are down about life. And please know that being in a financial rut *will* leave you feeling down on life. Just remember to take care of yourself, and don't forget that the rest of people your age are most likely going through the exact same thing. Below are some alternatives to help you live more simply and save a few bucks along the way.

INEXPENSIVE ADVENTURES

Sally-Spender Activities	Stanley-Saver Alternatives
Go to Barnes and Noble, blow money on the latest fiction books—even career-based books—and toss in a large latte.	Head over to the public library to check out books. Use career resources there and take a few personal-interest books out. Stop for a small latte on the way home.
Hit the bar with friends for a night out. Have dinner and a few drinks.	Hit the bar with friends for a night out. Eat dinner at home before you go and have a drink or two at the bar.

Go out after work for dinner with coworkers.	Go out to a restaurant that has happy hour specials with coworkers.
Cruise over to the cinema to see the latest movie on the night it comes out.	Cruise over to the cinema for a matinee.
Escape out of your office on your lunch break to the deli down the road.	Pack your lunch and bring it with you when you bust out of the fluorescent light for a nice lunch outside.

Hopefully, you can see that the chart is just a guide to illustrate the difference in ways to cut back while still allowing yourself to have fun during this exciting phase in your life. You will no doubt think of other ways to save money while still feeding your soul that you can add to the chart.

Sean Harvey, a New York-based career consultant we've heard from throughout the book, says self-care is a huge consideration. "It's critical to take time out for yourself to recharge, especially if you have a demanding job and an active social life," he says. Harvey adds that overlooking self-care can easily lead to burn-out in a couple of years. "It's important to be mindful of the balance in your life: your level of commitment to your job; the quality of your social life; the variety of activities you're taking advantage of while you're home; and the amount of alone time you have without being connected to a computer and cell phone," he adds. So now that you know taking time for yourself is important—and that you can do it without spending a ton—what are you waiting for? These may not feel like the best times of your life, but there's no harm in kicking back a little and having some good ol' 20-something fun!

Good Credit, Bad Debt

Paycheck to paycheck seemed to be the norm for many recent grads. But as many people moved through their early- to mid-20s, most of them picked up some financial wisdom along the way. Julie-Ann, whom we heard from earlier in this chapter, is the perfect example. She supported herself through school and graduated with the debt to prove it.

"I definitely live paycheck to paycheck and sometimes it's rough. I have to seriously consider every purchase, and it sometimes feels unfair when so many of my friends can afford to go out for fancy dinners without thinking about it at all," says Julie-Ann. "I often have to use my cards as a crutch to buy basic things like gas or food each month."

While she does have a large amount of credit card debt, Julie-Ann has excellent credit. Why? She's learned how to manage her credit. Because it's not possible to pay her entire debt load off in a lump sum, she makes regular payments—always on time. That's key to creating a positive out of an otherwise negative situation. Because really, it's easy to think about getting rid of debt. But you have to learn how to live *with* it for a while in most cases. Even though Julie-Ann owes quite a bit of money, she has been responsible with payments to avoid ruining her credit. I'm confident that she'll get that debt paid off and that she'll be rewarded, should she go to buy a house one day or something like that. That's what good credit will do for her.

So what does this wise girl say about living with credit card debt? "If you have more than one credit card, cut all of them up except one. Use it for necessities, not desires. Buy groceries, not dinner for your friends. Pay your electric bill, don't buy shoes," Julie-Ann says. While I'm sure she'd rather not have the debt she has accrued, I wanted to highlight how she managed to work *with* her financial situation and how she's making the best of it. "It's okay to have and use a credit card right out of college, but just use it wisely and always pay at least the minimum. Even if you owe a lot of money, you want to be in good standing with creditors," Julie-Ann concludes.

Paying off Your Student Loans

Whether or not your student loan is the only debt you have emerging out of college, it's important to understand how to pay off those bills. I remember going through "Exit Counseling" when I graduated college. I got to speak to a loan specialist and review my options. You can have set payments or opt for a graduated pay-back plan where your payments increase every few years (this assumes your income will too!) I'm not a financial expert, which is why I'm including some commentary from professionals who can give you advice. But I do know that loan companies are very flexible and can work with you to devise a solution that will help you pay off your college debt.

Julie-Ann took another smart approach to paying off her student loans. "I knew from the beginning that I wouldn't have tons of money right away, so I opted for the graduated pay-back plan. Every two years my minimum payment has been raised by about $25 and that has worked out well for me," she explains. I actually did the same thing, and that worked for me also. I am still pecking away at the debt.

Is Consolidation the Key?

According to the website Debt Help, nearly 78 percent of students do not know how deeply they are in debt from attending college and tend to underestimate that amount by approximately $5,000. With a large amount of debt, it is most likely spread out over several loans. That's why many students I interviewed were happy to hear about the concept of consolidating their college loans; that is, combining them into one loan with one payment.

I called upon John Turner, Debt Help's president, to give some financial advice about consolidating. First, he says students and graduates need to be aware of their financial options for paying back their loans, especially when they emerge out of college and tend to not make a lot of money. Every penny counts in this kind of predicament, literally. "One of the best options for getting some relief and avoiding default is to consolidate school loans," explains Turner. "You can get lower interest rates and monthly payments, and you can also extend payment years. You may even qualify for deferment or loan forgiveness. It's just a matter of learning about the different options available."

Turner says that both federal student loans and private student loans can be consolidated but advises against consolidating them together. "This is because there are many benefits to federal loans that may be lost should they be combined with a private loan," he explains. The good news about consolidating federal student loans is that the process is available to just about anyone, and it doesn't require any collateral or a co-signer. Some companies might require that the borrower have a minimum amount of student debt in order to quality, such as $10,000, Turner concludes.

Turner explains that consolidating federal student loans may provide borrowers with some benefits. Here are some of the perks of consolidation:

- ❍ The opportunity to lock in a low interest rate for the life of the loan

- ❍ A longer repayment period that allows for lower monthly payments

- ❍ The simplification of having only one student loan bill to pay per month

- ❍ Flexible choices for repayment

- ❍ An improved credit score by closing one or more open accounts

When it comes to consolidating private student loans, Turner recommends it. Although the benefits may not be as far-reaching as federal loan consolidation, he notes that consolidating private student loans can assist graduates in the following ways:

- ❍ Simplify finances significantly

- ❍ Improve the borrower's credit score by closing one or more open accounts

- ❍ Lower interest rates

With so many financial professionals and companies pushing for consolidation, you may wonder if it's good for all grads. "While consolidation of federal student loans is recommended for the majority of students, there are situations in which it might be preferable to keep loans separate," Turner reveals. "This might be the case if a borrower has a loan with special privileges attached. Once loans are consolidated, the individual loans are gone and so then are the benefits attached to them." The federal Perkins loan, for example, gives borrowers with specific opportunities a loan forgiveness that would be lost if such a loan were consolidated. "This is not to say that one should not include such a loan in consolidation, but rather that borrowers should weigh the pros and cons of consolidation carefully if they have loans with special benefits attached," Turner concludes. In other words, talk to your lender and explore your options. I'll discuss how to do that later in this chapter.

Deferment vs. Forbearance

Let's toss in a few more terms that every fiscally responsible adult should know: deferment and forbearance. Especially if you have loans, it's good to understand how loans work, including how they provide flexible repayment options. Heather Graskewicz, a certified financial counselor at GreenPath Debt Solutions, says a typical student's credit report includes a dozen or so student loan accounts from the same lender with varying balances. Some may be Stafford loans, Perkins loans or other federal loans. That's why she recommends consolidating after school. "Consolidating is an excellent way to reign in the various loans and have one monthly payment. By consolidating, a student may also be able to obtain a lower interest rate," she says.

Graskewicz explains that most student loan payments are deferred for six months after graduation. This means that you don't pay anything the first six months. During this period, your loans will not accrue interest, she adds. Of course once your six months is up, the lenders expect payments. So is six months all you get? Not quite. "If the student is experiencing financial difficulty at any point in repayment, he or she may request forbearance or another deferment," Graskewicz says. Forbearance is similar to a deferment in the respect that you won't have to make payments for a period of time. But unlike deferment, your loan *will* accrue interest. While forbearances are relatively easy to obtain, they're not a long-term solution.

Graskewicz confides that she used forbearance with her own loans. "My husband and I ran into some financial problems, and I chose to put my student loans into forbearance. At that time, my loans were through the U.S. Department of Education, and all I needed to do was submit an online request. I simply needed to select a reason why

I needed the forbearance and choose the length of time, and then I received notification in the mail that my request had been approved," she explains. Graskewicz further notes that an individual's eligibility for forbearance is determined by the lender, and not all people are able to get forbearance. "I have spoken with several clients who had private student loans and were not allowed forbearance at any point, regardless of the situation. With lenders who permit forbearances, there are limitations to the number of times a loan can be placed into forbearance—even Uncle Sam has his limits," she concludes. I too recall using forbearance about a year after I graduated. While I was making more money in my second job, my rent was higher and living on my own created pressures—as did the credit card debt I had at the time.

So, to get it straight, borrowers have several options, as outlined by Turner and Graskewicz. In conclusion, let's consider conditions/situations that qualify students for the option of deferment. Turner says you can defer—or postpone—repayment of federal student loans for several different reasons:

○ The borrower is enrolled at a post-secondary institution at least half-time. (Deferment on these grounds may last indefinitely.)

○ The borrower is unable to secure full-time employment. (Deferment on these grounds may last up to three years.)

○ The borrower is enduring economic hardship. (Deferment on these grounds may last up to three years.)

Turner notes that the federal Perkins loan allows for deferment—even debt forgiveness—in other situations. For example, he says, repayment of a Perkins loan might be deferred or forgiven if the borrower is a full-time teacher at a designated school for low-income families, if the borrower is a full-time employee of a social agency for low-income families, or if the borrower serves in the armed forces. "In order to secure deferment on a federal student loan, the borrower must formally request such action. Private student loans are not eligible for deferment," Turner adds.

Working with Your Lender

There's something to be said about the student loan lenders. While you may have to wait on the phone or go through a confusing maze of "Press 1 . . . Press 2 . . . Press 3" to talk to a loan specialist, they are worth the wait. In my experience, and in light of what many students have confided, loan professionals can help you determine what options are best for you.

"In general, companies that offer student loans are very flexible when it comes to repayment," Turner says. This is because loan companies do not want student borrowers to go into default on their debts, so most are willing to work with individuals who find themselves in difficult financial situations. Turner explains that there are four different flexible repayment plans for federal student loans from which borrowers may choose:

○ *Standard Repayment:* The borrower makes fixed monthly payments throughout the term of the loan, for a period up to 10 years.

○ *Extended Repayment:* The borrower makes fixed monthly payments throughout the term of the loan, but for 12 to 30 years instead of the standard 10 years. This translates into smaller monthly payments.

○ *Graduated Repayment:* With this option, repayment increments start small and increase gradually every two years, for a 12- to 30-year loan term.

○ *Income Contingent Repayment:* The monthly payments are based on the borrower's income and may change from year to year as income changes, for a loan term of up to 25 years. When the loan term is up, any remaining debt is discharged (forgiven).

Again, if you find that you are unable to make the payments as required by the repayment plan, forbearance may be requested. It's not a long-term answer, but it's a great saver if you run into a temporary financial catastrophe. Remember to talk to your lender about this if you're having difficulty with repayment. "Most lenders will be more than willing to work with such pro-active borrowers," Turner adds.

Saving for Retirement and Investing

So I'll admit: Thinking about retirement as a recent graduate sounds kind of odd. When I graduated from college, I was more concerned about finding a job and paying rent than saving money for when I was old and gray. I know it sounds far off, but if you save a little now for retirement, it will pay off in the future.

Luckily, most companies offer 401(k) programs. I remember starting mine just to get my mother off my back. I put in $5 a week. The amount was so low that my boss at the time matched the whole amount. The great thing was that I was saving $10 a week—and the amount was tax deductible. I've continued my small retirement fund and admit that I should be putting more away. But at least I have the account!

That's why I wanted to talk about saving for retirement and investing in this chapter. Because as far off as it may sound for many graduates, it's a viable option with big payoffs—sometimes literally! Of course I'm no Suze Orman (but *do* check out her books) so I've called in another expert to weigh in on saving up.

To begin, you may wondering if it's smarter to pay back loans before you even think of saving or investing. Chuck Saletta, a contributor to The Motley Fool, a financial and investment services company based in Virginia, says it depends what kind of loan you have when it comes to repayment versus saving. "Generally speaking, the rule of thumb is to aggressively pay back any loan that is not for an appreciating asset, like a home or an education, one that is at higher interest rate than you can reasonably achieve by investing the money instead of paying back the debt after considering taxes, or one that carries 'gotcha' terms like a spiking higher interest rate, or a nasty balloon payment at the end," he says. "Stock investments should be for longer-term priorities," Saletta continues. "If you know you're going to spend money tomorrow or next year, you should be saving the money you're planning to spend on that item in something a little more stable like a CD, money market fund, or even a savings account." For our purposes, let's focus on the savings aspect. There are plenty of resources for investing, including Saletta's Web site at www.themotleyfool.com.

So, what about 401(k)s—are they really necessary at this point? Saletta offers some pointers about having a 401(k), excluding information on the new Roth 401(k), which isn't too common yet. He says the traditional 401(k) offers employees the chance to put in money and have their employers match that amount. But—of course there's a "but"!—employers do limit what they contribute, and you will get penalized if you take out that money before it is matched. Saletta says that matching limits from employers are set by the government, but companies have broad options when it comes to 401(k)s. He has seen some matches starting as high as $3 for $1 on the first 1 percent of a person's salary. The most typical match he has seen is $0.50 per $1, up to 6% of a person's salary, he adds.

"401(k)s are great things to have—for people who participate in them. If you don't participate though, they're rather useless," Saletta says. "The thing is, the time value of money really kicks into play with 401(k)s. Early money is worth far, far more than late money. At a 10% compounded rate of return, $2,000 invested at age 20 is worth about the same as $90,000 invested at age 60. As painful as it may be to invest early, those early dollars can actually make up the bulk of someone's ultimate retirement benefit." When it comes to investing, a 401(k) is a great start. "Saving and investing money has to be a priority, but it doesn't have to be painful," adds Saletta. "As the example above showed, a little bit of money invested early can more than make up for a whole lot of cash saved later."

Saletta also shared a few tips to help college grads put away a few bucks:

○ Pay yourself first. As soon as you're hired (or are eligible), sign up for 401(k) contributions to come straight out of your paycheck. You don't miss money you never see.

○ Invest one half of each raise. If you were living comfortably on what you were making before your raise, this lets you get some of your reward for your hard work today, while still saving money for the future. Best of all, since it came from new income, rather than existing income, you won't even feel the initial sting, he says.

○ Take advantage of free money. Seriously. If you get a 50 percent match on your 401(k) and you're in the 25-percent tax bracket, the net result of contributing to your traditional 401(k) is that you get $2 worth of invested cash in your account for every $1 worth of spendable cash you invest.

○ Make simple choices. Many offices have free coffee or "coffee clubs" where $5 and taking a turn making a pot will get you all the coffee you need for a month. Either way, it's a heck of a lot cheaper than running out to Starbucks. If soda provides your caffeine of choice, buying two-liters or even individual serving bottles from a grocery store is usually a lot cheaper than buying cans from a vending machine.

○ Brown bag your lunch. Leftover dinners make wonderful brown-bagged lunches. Heck, I don't know the last time I specifically made lunch for myself, but I brown bag my lunch probably four times a week. It's usually leftovers from the night before.

○ Time shift to avoid rush hour. If I drive to work during rush hour, I need a new tank of gas every five to six working days. If I manage my time around rush hour, I can usually go seven to eight days. That adds up to about one to two avoided tanks of gas every month.

○ Speaking of the car, "safe, reliable transportation" has to be the primary purpose of any budget-minded person's car, Saletta says. "Gently used" vehicles can last almost as long as a new car, for a far lower up-front cost. A flashy sports car is fine if you've already hit the big time, but if you're truly struggling to make ends meet, the payment, insurance and gas costs all add up to extra expenses you could have otherwise lived without.

○ Mass transit works wonders, if the schedule is convenient. No parking costs, no gas costs, no wear-and-tear on the car. Carpooling works too, if you've got coworkers on similar schedules.

○ In the same vein as my lunches...Cook enough for several meals at once. Freeze or refrigerate what you don't eat right away and call it lunch, dinner, etc. some other day. Eating out can be a huge budget killer, but we've found that we can eat very well for a very low total price per person per meal, thanks to things like buying value-size packs, cooking with the eye of having leftovers, etc.

○ Make sure to budget fun spending money. It's almost impossible to go cold turkey on entertainment spending—and almost nobody would really want to live that way. But if you give yourself $50 or $100 or something like that a month in entertainment cash, it makes it easier to stick with the rest of the program.

○ Avoid finance charges. If you can't afford to pay cash for something, you can't afford to pay it off over time at 19.99% interest, even if the monthly payments seem low. If having "stuff" is important to you, the truth is that you can actually buy more stuff over time by paying cash than you can by financing things, thanks to the interest charges.

Financial Warning

Michael Edesses, investment industry insider and author of *The Big Investment Lie: What Your Financial Advisor Doesn't Want You to Know*, encourages students to beware of financial professionals. Now, I know that I told you earlier how helpful lending representatives were to me. Even though that's true, it's good to use a little caution with anything you do.

"Financial professionals are in business to make money for themselves, and a lot of that money is made by charging big fees and super-high interest rates on credit card debt when they can get away with it. Believing they are in business to serve you, without regard to their own payoff, is a big mistake. Unfortunately, these facts are probably not taught well in college," Edesses says.

I don't want to go into the what-ifs of dealing with financial professionals. Right now, you're probably going to be conversing with your loan lender—not taking risky investments—so your risk of losing unnecessary money to a financial institution is probably low. Just use common sense if you choose to do anything chancy, such as investing. While investing is highly profitable, it's not good to get involved if you don't know much about it.

Even though I'm not a financial whiz, I have my own financial warning to pass on to you. This is a sign that will tell you when you've really hit rock bottom, can't pass 'go' and can't collect the $200. If you have to *charge* Ramen noodles, then it's time to get help. Seriously. Bad carbs should never put you into debt. College is okay, but not bad carbs!

TIPS >>

Staying Financially Healthy After College

Here are some tips on staying financially healthy after graduation from Sean Harvey, a career consultant at Boerum Consulting, based in New York.

Make a budget. This should be based on your realistic income after taxes and your realistic expenses that you spend in a given month.

Pay yourself first. Be sure you are setting money aside for your long-term financial planning. This can be as little as say $25 a month into your company's retirement planning programs. The money can add up quickly, especially when it's an automatic deduction and you're not thinking about it. Include the savings in your budgeting.

Create a financial cushion. Try to put additional money aside into a savings account that you only use in case of emergencies. You should aim to build up to three to six months of your monthly expenses into this account in case of emergencies, such as losing a job, paying for a health issue that's not covered by insurance or having to pay an unexpected expense that you didn't see coming.

Get insurance. Make sure that you have health insurance that is provided by your job, your professional association, any number of new health insurance plans out there for freelancers, or under your parents' plan. Unexpected health costs can derail financial planning if you're not protected.

Manage your debt. Try to take every advantage that your student loan companies give you to bring down your student loan debt by paying on time, paying electronically, and managing your debt responsibly. In terms of credit card debt, pay your credit card companies every month and don't miss a payment or be late. Don't take out more credit cards than you need.

CHAPTER 9
Having a Social Life

"I can still party all night . . . right?"

Whenever I think about all the angst I went through in my 20s, one thing sticks out: that darn environmental science degree. I mean, what was I thinking? . . . a right-brainer who intentionally went into a technical education field and struggled every bit of the way. Still today, people ask me why I studied in the sciences. My response? I was too busy having fun in college. It's true. While I was interested in environmental science and envisioned myself working for the state making policies and enforcing laws, I didn't think much more about my major once I started college. Something else took precedence.

That something was Circle K, a collegiate organization that enabled me to help others via community service. Through my work with Circle K, I met friends that I still have to this day. Even though Circle K received more of my college focus than my major, I don't blame this organization for my confusion about my career during my early 20s. For one thing, part of life after school is normally being in a state of uncertainty. But truth be told, I put Circle K before everything when I was in college. As much as students are focused on learning, making that the main goal of college, social development is a huge facet of the college experience—and one that can lead to a sense of loss after graduation when it's gone.

In high school I was a member of Key Club and had managed to get on the state board for more than 150 clubs in the state. Needless to say, my senior year of high school was fantastic because I traveled the country, met new people and made a difference at the same time. Going into college, I wanted more of the same. I joined the service organization Circle K, the college level of Kiwanis. (Yes, the same Kiwanis that usually has those circular signs with a huge "K" in the middle when you cross a town border and are welcomed into a new municipality.)

I immediately jumped into the Circle K organization at Stockton during 1996. My chapter had about six members, which grew to 40 by the beginning of my sophomore year when I took the helm as the club's president. That was when it really started. I began to develop close friends—the kind they say you'll meet in college but I hadn't my first year. During this time, the young man that was the state governor, Brian, was killed. It was a huge tragedy, but it propelled me even more to want to serve at a higher level. Once more, I attempted to get elected to the state board as governor. The first time I failed and subsequently returned to my club. They were a team of 40+ friends that made something of that little Pine Barrens-based school. When the rest of our classmates took off for the weekend at our suitcase school, we stuck around and got involved in things like picking up litter along streets and in waterways, and serving food to the needy in nearby Atlantic City.

This club had a buzz on campus as a group of people who *really* did something. If you ask me, I think Circle K brought a sense of camaraderie to the Stockton campus, boosting student involvement. The people in our club were active and we all had a great time doing campus activities, attending state-wide functions—and even traveling to places like Chicago, Jamaica and San Diego for international conventions. Stockton's club even garnered several district and international awards—far from its unknown status when the club had only six members.

My point is that by the time I ran for governor a second time, my club was behind me. It was because of them that I was elected and because of them that I achieved a major dream in my life. Not only had I envisioned serving on the state level in a Kiwanis organization, but I also wanted to pick up where Brian had left off and restore the state level to what it was when he was at the top. When I assumed the role of governor, the team I built at Stockton came with me. That year was the best in my life, one that I fondly recall.

With all the satisfaction I gained from being in Circle K—and all the activities I was involved in—academics took second place. I don't regret that because you can only learn so much in school to prepare you for life in the real world. For me, college was about more than getting a degree—it was about living—and *that's* why it was so hard for me to leave. That's why I faced a huge letdown when that part of my life was over. That's why I have an interest in college-aged students' issues. I'll be the first to admit that losing social ties—and even the act of leaving the place they originated—can be devastating. It was for me.

Before we begin, I want to note that those friends—those wonderful souls who brought me more pride than I can put into words—have stayed in my life. So while leaving Circle K was difficult, I still have its most important assets at my side as my very best friends today. They've been with me through my quarterlife crisis, stuck by my side as I built my career, crashed on my futon, and even witnessed my wedding. (Oh, and you should know that Circle K is how I met my husband, Tim. He was my secretary when I served as governor. How cute, right?) My point is that while you may go through an adjustment with your social life and have to work at maintaining friendships, it is possible to take the best parts of college with you when you go.

Internet Friends

Jessica, who we heard from in Chapter 3, was never much of a social butterfly. "I have a few friends I talk to regularly, but I don't think you'd even call us best friends or anything like that. I care deeply for the people around me, but we all seem to keep to our personal space a lot as well," she confides. While she keeps in touch more so with friends from high school, she has lost touch with a lot of college buddies. (But it should be said that she went from college in London back home to life in Scotland, so that is definitely a defining factor.)

Still, she says the Internet is helpful when keeping in touch. "With my friends in London, I use text messages mostly, we write to each other sometimes, and I try to go see as many of them as I can whenever I'm in the city." As for meeting new friends, she has met new pals over the Internet by subscribing to interest groups focused on two of her hobbies—cult TV and history. She has even met a few Internet friends in person too. It just goes to show that the only way to meet new people *isn't* by hitting the bars (though that can be fun!).

Looking Forward to Looking Back?

Susan has managed to stay in touch with college friends and reports that she is even more socially active since graduating. She's visited pals along the East Coast and uses email, text messages and the phone to stay in touch. But she admits that sometimes it is hard to keep old friends because people develop and evolve with the passing of time. "The thing about college friends is that things can change really quickly after graduation. People get engaged, move home, or get a $100K job in investment banking, and suddenly you have nothing in common." While Susan says she embraced life after college as she started working full-time and attending networking events, many of her friends were hanging out at the same college bars, spending time on campus, and sticking around to attend graduate school. "Nothing against that way of life," Susan notes, "but I needed friends who were more mature and understood the adult world."

Even though Susan maintained college friendships, she still managed to create new relationships too. "I found it really hard to meet people at first, because suddenly I was no longer surrounded by people my own age with lots of low-cost activities on campus. I wish I'd stopped dwelling on this and gotten out there sooner," she comments. Susan believes that living in a big city—she lives in Boston—is the perfect place to get "out there." She recommends taking an adult educa-tion class, going to a young professionals' mixer, volunteering, joining company sports teams, or getting a gym membership. "If you live in the 'burbs, it might be harder but not impossible."

Leah, whom we met in Chapters 3 and 7, says that she *makes* time to keep in touch with her friends. Still, she feels she is less social now than college because she is busy working as a nurse in Boston. "I have a full-time job and more responsibilities. I try to go out at least once a week and I spend a lot of time with my boyfriend, but it's really some-thing I have to work on. I don't have the energy that I used to, and I get so tired after going out and drinking just one night. And if I stay up late, it throws off my sleeping for a few days," she explains. "In college I felt like I recovered so much faster," Leah laments. True that. I don't know what happens to working adults—maybe it's the monotony of the working world or the crazy schedules—but so many of my friends and I joked about how old we felt when we were just 22!

Leah brings a different perspective about friendships after college. She says she's not sure if she will make any more lifelong friends be-cause she plans on moving. "I have a couple of friends I have made here in the past year whom I would like to keep in touch with," she shares. But Leah said at the time of publication that she was planning on moving to the West Coast in a year. "I think it was easier to make friends in college where everyone is your age and going through the same college classes and schedules and interested in the same campus activities," she adds.

But Leah realizes the importance of making friends. "I could never be cut off from my old friends from high school or college, but it is so important to open up to new friends, especially co-workers whom you spend so much time with each week." While you may think she's a little closed-minded about making more good friends at such a young age, I think it's easy to understand her position—especially considering her impending move. It's hard to plant roots when you're on the go.

I recall feeling the same way about friends after graduation, and most of my college friends were within an hour's drive. Although I haven't met many new friends I would consider having for the rest

of my life, I have been able to deepen certain relationships and create better friendships with school acquaintances upon graduation. It's
different for everyone, but it's always good to open yourself up to the
possibility that new friends are out there, and that it is never too late to
meet a permanent pal.

Putting Yourself Out There

Sara, a Kent State University graduate, enjoys a mix of friendships with
her college pals and new buddies. "I always want to meet new people
and I think lifelong friendships can start at any point, whether you're
21 or 81. You always have to keep yourself open to friendships," she
comments. Upon listening to Sara talk, I had to admit that I was a
little jealous. When I graduated, I wasn't too focused on meeting new
people, as I adored my college friends. Now I'm more open to new
friendships although I realize they can't replace the old. But it's definitely vital to always have new people come into your life—especially
because you're going to be going through so many phases during the
years that are ahead, so it's good to have friends who support those
phases, as well as those who are more long term.

Sara, now married, has made friends with people in her apartment
development. "They saw inside our apartment when they first moved
in, thought it looked nice (and assumed we were nice people), so they
knocked on our door," she recalls. "I definitely think it's all about putting yourself out there." She advises meeting up with coworkers and
joining professional organizations. In addition, Sara enjoys the Internet
to meet people, and recommends starting a blog or using MySpace to
connect with others. "Once you put yourself out there, you'd be surprised at how many people are in the exact same boat as you. So don't
be afraid to smile at the person you pass every day at work, but you've
never stopped to get to know."

Emily, who graduated from Boston University, says she is less social since she graduated with her English degree. "Now that everyone
has to work, we're exhausted by 11 p.m. and need to sleep," she says.
"It's more a special occasion when a bunch of friends make the effort

to hang out now. Of course, we do like our trips to the bar for a few drinks just to relax." Emily keeps in touch with friends and says she's learned to recognize who her friends are based on proximity, and who her friends are based on personal connections. The same is true of high school, she notes. She uses Facebook.com and MySpace.com to keep in touch with friends and adds she has also reunited with friends in person.

While it's clear to see that Emily will make lifelong friends throughout her life, she admits that it's easier to meet people in a large environment such as college. "There is a certain bond you gain when your friendship with someone was forged while you were both still really young and in a transitional childhood-to-adulthood situation," she says.

The Changing Face of Dating

When it comes to dating, Emily defines herself as a "serial monogamist" who constantly finds herself in relationships without having any intention of getting into one. "I had to try very hard to be single after a string of exhausting relationships, and I really loved that time to answer only to myself and to get to know my friends better than I had when all the needy exes were taking my time and attention," she says. Of course, times are changing. While she's not ready for marriage, Emily says that it's not an unthinkable option since she graduated, especially since friends her age are starting to settle down.

Lacey, a graduate of Colorado State University, is in a similar situation. She reports that she is less social since completing her undergraduate education. Hopefully during graduate school her personal life will pick up a little. But when it comes to dating, she is not trying to initiate anything. "I'm not looking for a serious relationship currently because I'm trying to keep my mind open for grad school. I have tried serious relationships since I graduated, and they aren't working," explains Lacey, who instructs community college students on developmental writing. In fact, she says that she's not sure if she's ready to date again. "I think I'm still growing up in unseen/unseeable ways, and so are many of the people I date," she confides. Lacey says she isn't sure how to compare dating after college to dating in college either. "I feel like I'm going about it in the same way, just with fewer groups of people to choose from," she concludes.

Getting Serious

Meredith, a St. Olaf College graduate, is currently in a relationship. Graduating hasn't made her want it to be something serious, although she admits she has always viewed dating as an opportunity to find something true and long lasting. "Now more than before though, it's comforting to put effort into finding someone you want to make a commitment to. Plus, it makes cooking a lot easier," she says. "Seriously though, for me it's something important that I find I'm wanting more and more now that I'm on my own."

Some people aren't as serious about dating, or as intent on finding a partner for life that early in their lives. When I dated in college, it was never to find something serious but more about getting to know other people and experiencing emotions. Even after I graduated, I wasn't intent on getting married right away. Of course when I met my husband, it created quite a stir because I knew he was marriage material.

Ashley, a Kent State University Ohio graduate, has a story similar to mine. She didn't get serious with anyone while dating during college. But her senior year, she met someone special whom she thinks she will someday marry. "I don't think I would have been ready for this relationship if I had not experienced new things in college and been free to do what I wanted," says Ashley, adding that dating during college helped to show her what she wanted in a mate and helped her develop the skills needed in maintaining a strong relationship. I guess that's the point of dating—learning about what you do and don't want from a partner and having a good time. While some recent grads are ready to settle down, others continue to date and to enjoy meeting new people; it's all a matter of preference.

The Quad Syndrome

If you're anything like I was when I graduated, you are probably on the less sociable side, wanting to hang on to the old, feeling that you've met your lifelong friends and don't need to reach out for more. While that may be true, I ask you to open your mind to meeting new people. Why, you may ask? Let's call it "Quad Syndrome." I think this is safe to say, as every college I know has a quad, or at least a hub where students hang. Mine did. It was surrounded by pine trees and had a volleyball court. It served as the center between both dormitories and was a fun gathering place to hang out. Thing is, once it was gone from my life, I was bummed.

The Quad Syndrome isn't about being upset that you aren't at your college quad. It wasn't even about being a social butterfly when you were there. You didn't have to be the most popular student on campus to experience it either. It's more than that, folks. You see, at college, you had everything you needed. Education—check. A place to live—check. Semi-decent food—check. Friends—check. You were surrounded in this little incubator, if you will, where a community existed. That community shifted the day you put on your cap and gown...that day you drove off with your last load of dirty laundry (which was fresh for Mom to wash when you got home, degree in tote).

The point is that when you graduate, you leave your community behind. Even if you didn't physically hang out in the quad, you were a part of the interdependence. The population may have changed somewhat from semester to semester; but generally, just because it is the nature of college life, things were much the same. You could count on that. So when your community was gone, and everything was not right there for you any more, you may have felt the loss. *This is the Quad Syndrome.* It's when you feel the loss brought on by leaving a close-knit community at college.

Let me be honest. I'm always going to have the Quad Syndrome. I'm always going to long to smell the scent of pine trees, and yes, I'll even look fondly back on *most* of my college classes. Just being there, a part of it all . . . learning. I'll always miss it. But I'm not yearning for it as much anymore. I think if you find new comforts, you'll be able to appreciate the old ones—and even revisit them—while looking toward the future. Of course every now and then if you're lucky enough to venture back to your college, I encourage you to do so. Sit in that quad. On your steps. Near that tree you loved. Be where you used to be and think about how far you've come. If you don't think anything has changed, go back in six months. My point is that it's okay to miss college, or to miss whatever it represented to you. Like losing a loved one, I think college is a time in your life that has to be mourned. But do . . . please *do* look ahead.

In with the Old, In with the New

As I told you before, I found it hard to leave college. Even though my closest friends are those I've known the longest, I have personally had to make strides to meet new people. I wanted fresh folks to hang out with, and I have found that I grow more from knowing others. Other college grads have found the same thing.

Rachel, a graduate of the University of Southern California, keeps her mind open when it comes to meeting people. She feels it's become kind of easy to meet new friends, as she reports having more time now that she has graduated. "I have found myself to be more social now that I am through with college. I do not have to go home to do homework, or have weird working hours because of labs. I get my work done and then I can go out and do what I want," Rachel comments.

While she's kept in touch with some college friends, Rachel makes it a point not to cling to the past. "We are who we are today because of the people from our past, but meeting new people allows us to learn new things about ourselves today. It is great having those around you that you know you can trust and confide in, but it is vital that you also have an inflow of new people in order to make sure that you are growing as a person." Rachel enjoys meeting new people, and has a pool of friends that run the gamut from kindergarten pals to new buddies she is still getting to know. "College is by no means the only time to make life-long friends. People come and go . . . friends come and go . . . that is life. I can't think that the people I meet from here on out will not play a major role in the rest of my life. Only time can tell me that."

Another plus to being a social butterfly is using it to network. Rachel says she began networking during college. During a workshop at her school's career lab, she learned that networking was a great way to get what she wanted out of life. "If you know enough people and you know how to work the right contacts, you may be able to find a job or get yourself into a position that will help you in the future that you may not have been able to get otherwise," adds Rachel.

While networking is a great bonus to being social, it's not the focus of this chapter. I wanted to expose you to the thoughts and stories of those, just like you, who have graduated and are facing social challenges and other related issues. Maybe your job is going great, and you're not having problems making ends meet. But we can't deny that the change in social climate is real. Whether your social life booms after school or lulls—or you experience Quad Syndrome—social aspects are a huge deal for recent grads. Heck, friendships—and relationships, romantic or not, in general—are the very essence of life and love. When they change, it can be difficult to cope with, so I hope some of the stories here have helped you identify with others. Before we end, I'll share one more, from an interviewee who maturely summed up the spirit of our social lives after college and throughout the rest of our lives.

Meredith says that she's had to make more of an effort to maintain her friendships since graduating. She admits to being more of a homebody, content to stay in for the night and bake cookies rather than going out to glam it up around town. "Now that I'm living on my own though and don't see my friends at meals, in class, or in passing, it means I must make more of an effort to get out and meet up with them," she says. Luckily, most of her friends live in the same area. But she still keeps up with those who don't, using the phone, email and good old fashioned mail to stay in touch.

So what about getting out there and adding some new pals to the mix? "I'm a very strong believer in both keeping old friends and making new ones," Meredith shares. "It's definitely not easy to do either of them, but well worth the effort. My old friends know me in ways that new friends do not; we have inside jokes, share so many stories, and have been through a lot together. But making new friends is so much fun and keeps life interesting and exciting," she says. Meredith adds that as individuals grow, work and live, they have the opportunity to meet new people. "If we don't take advantage of that, I think we're missing out on knowing some incredible people who could have a huge impact on us," she adds. Good point. While this is an exciting time of your life with regard to your independence, you can always use a good buddy to get you through the not-so-great moments that can surprise you.

Sparking It Up: Meeting New Peeps

There are plenty of ways for recent graduates to meet new people. Of course there are interesting people to get to know at your job. There are also a slew of recreational activities to partake in. Have a biking hobby? Join a cycling group! Like to knit? Go to a Stitch 'n Bitch session. Want to hang back and interact? Hop on the Internet! You get the point!

Meredith, the St. Olaf College graduate we've heard from already, suggests joining a volunteer or church organization. "They're nice because you automatically have something in common with them you can talk about," she says. "But even the grocery store is a place you can meet people, especially if you see and run into the same people often. If you go out to bars or clubs, you probably want to censor and screen a little more, but that's a venue for new people too."

While some graduates stay away from the bar scene, others don't mind. It's just a matter of personal preference when it comes to what activities you like. But most grads did agree that getting out was key to making new friends. "I think you do have to be willing to put yourself out there at least a little bit if you're really serious about it, but there will be new people everywhere you go, so the opportunities are right there waiting to be had," Meredith adds.

Dave still manages to have an active social life since he graduated from Villanova University in Pennsylvania, but he suggests that things are different now. He still has fun on a more mature level compared to his wild college nights spent drinking with friends. But he's satisfied overall with how his social life has turned out during a time when most friends are losing touch with their buddies in pursuit of their dream jobs.

What's made the difference for Dave? He initiated staying involved. He joined a few soccer teams and even signed up for a whiffle ball league. He also can afford to go into Philadelphia often to spend time with people that he knows from his job. Living with two college buddies helps—he still has social interaction, which can ease the transition into the working world that is so difficult for many graduates. (Trust me on that . . . I spent the first six months of my working life coming home to an empty apartment every night.) By living with roommates, you have someone to talk to and you can cut down on rent.

For Dave, keeping in touch with his college friends has been pretty easy. He relies on email, text messages, his cell phone and even fantasy football leagues. "I've made a bunch of new friends through work, sports leagues, friends-of-friends, etc. But I've also been able to maintain college friendships—even high school friendships—mainly because it's so easy to communicate." I like Dave's balance because he stays in touch with old friends and realizes it is important to make new ones too.

Sara, whom we heard from in Chapter 2, says there are plenty of ways to meet new friends after college. She and her husband found good friends in their neighbors. "Talk to people in line at Starbucks. Join professional organizations. Ask your co-workers if they want to go out after work. Follow a local band. The Internet is also a great place to meet people in your area. Start a blog. Join MySpace.com. Check out Craigslist.com," she says.

Getting Environmentally Friendly

Sometimes, your social life lies in your environment, and in some cases, meeting new friends won't be as much of a priority as greeting your new surroundings. Richard Marquis, a Michigan-based author, speaker and college success expert, has some good advice, even if you're working in the town in which you grew up.

"Why not make your new job and community environment a metaphor of your home town—perhaps even the ideal town in which you would like to live?" he asks. For example, Marquis recommends commencing with a comfortable routine in your new job and city. "Single out a reasonably priced restaurant, café, bookstore, etc. that you can call 'mine,'" he says. "Choose places that, from the minute you set foot inside the door, convey upbeat and comfortable vibes. Especially note those places where servers and other customers make you feel better for just being there," Marquis suggests. "For maximum benefit, make it fun and free. The idea is for you to more easily connect with your new world. Maybe there is a fountain that you can visit in the early evening at which you can read a book—or just be. You might choose to ride the bus to and from work, leisurely working your way through a favorite book."

He also suggests playing tourist in your city, including asking strangers questions about the local scene. Once assimilated to your new pad, you can join an organization focused on your career, personal, or romantic initiatives. "With each visit, you will notice familiar faces. With each event you attend, you will come to realize that even many of the locals do not know everybody. Introduce yourself to them at gatherings where food, conversation and sociability are served up—such as at spaghetti dinners, dances, fundraisers, etc. Not only are they usually inexpensive, they are often looking for volunteers to help out. What a great way to meet and know people more quickly—and with very little effort on your part," Marquis adds.

If you're feeling isolated, Marquis recommends doing some good deeds. "One of the best ways to get your mind off your sense of isolation in a new town is to strive to be kind to others in small ways," he says. "For example, the elder population is the fastest growing segment of our society. And they are the least likely to be exploitative of others—especially young, sympathetic adults. Why not take the time to interact with senior citizens? Not only will you feel less alone but don't be surprised if you enjoy the experience and feel better about yourself. You may even discover that they become the best friends of all. Although older adults are often overlooked in our youth-obsessed world, they have a great deal of unassuming wisdom, kindness and other-centeredness to offer. That alone is its own reward."

Regardless of how you do it, there are many ways to assimilate to social life during The After-College. We've talked about meeting new friends while hanging on to the old, getting used to a new town, and finding innovative ways to meet fresh pals. So maybe spending time with the elderly isn't your cup of tea. Or hanging out at the local coffeehouse isn't your cup of java. There are ways to continue having fun that will ensure you'll always have a friend to lean on during this crazy, thrilling and exciting time in your life.

CHAPTER 10

The Quarterlife Crisis

"Okay, this cannot be normal!"

Sometimes, The After-College can be so intense for grads that it turns into a "quarterlife crisis." This term is now a household name—and appropriately so—as what ensues after you get your diploma can be a real catastrophe. In their book *Quarterlife Crisis: The Unique Challenges of Life in Your Twenties,* authors Abby Wilner and Alexandra Robbins define "quarterlife crisis" as "a response to overwhelming instability, constant change, too many choices and a panicked sense of helplessness."

I do not believe that The After-College is the same thing as a quarterlife crisis. Rather, it should be said that you can go through a quarterlife crisis *during* The After-College. From the start, I've explained The After-College as the period in your life after college when you're settling into your adult and professional life. I think for too long, this period of time was automatically referred to as a quarterlife crisis. Not so, I think. While you can have crisis-like times during your After-College, the entire period shouldn't be doomed to a negative connotation—plenty of good things happen during The After-College too.

But we're not going to discuss many of the good things in this chapter since what we'll cover in the following pages is about *rock bottom*. You may hit it once. You may visit time and time and time again. You may never know what a quarterlife crisis is. In my opinion, many people don't know they're in a quarterlife crisis until they're in it. Then they hear the term and say, "Yep, that's what I'm going through!" The same thing happened to me when I read Wilner and Robbins' book. But it was a downturn for me at first—I associated all of my 20s as a crisis—until I figured out that it wasn't all a catastrophe. There were just parts that were emotionally, mentally and physically draining for me.

Whether you believe in this idea or not doesn't change the fact that transitioning into The After-College can be thrilling and horrifying at the same time. I went through my own quarterlife crisis. Before I regale you with stories of others' suffering, let me assure you that you can emerge successfully out of a crisis should you experience one.

Defining the QLC

When interviewing students for this book, I decided to first ask them how they defined the term "quarterlife crisis." (Since The After-College isn't a household name—yet—I couldn't really gauge what people thought of it.) While I got a variety of answers, most students nowadays know generally what it means to say someone is having a quarterlife crisis and many expect to experience their own sort of crisis at some point. Melissa, who graduated from Ohio University, defines the term "quarterlife crisis" as "when you hit your mid-twenties and become scared about where your life is heading, including your career, relationships and social life." She's pretty straight on.

Erika defined the concept of a quarterlife crisis as "a post-college 'What the hell am I supposed to do with my life now?' kind of thing." She says she believes that the theory of a crisis in one's 20s exists for a certain segment of people in a particular cultural place in time. Samantha, whom you heard from in Chapter 4, says she went through a quarterlife crisis and defines it as something pretty common. "[It's] what a lot of people go through in their 20s after college when they leave the stability and comfort of home and college life. They are suddenly on their own, trying to figure out who they are, where they fit, and [what to do with] all the options they have in front of them, which one to choose—and how. I went through it," she explains.

Andrea, who graduated from the University of Dallas with her Bachelor's degree and the University of West Georgia with her Master's degree, defined a quarterlife crisis as "an experience that occurs in the early- to mid-20s, usually after completing the standard cultural requirements to enter into society." She says after completing their education, many people experience confusion and desperation about the future. Andrea took her definition a step further (as most people who have studied young adults have) to include that feelings of depression, hopelessness and anxiety accompany the quarterlife crisis.

Even though my quarterlife crisis was, at times, a crisis, I wouldn't say the whole experience was. It was a natural growth process derived from graduating from college and entering the working world.

Crisis or not, there are several awkward, scary and downright shocking things that just about every grad goes through. Whether they experience depression or worry about their career direction, the quarterlife crisis entails going through a period of mental turmoil. On the same note though, you can go through a hard time and still find the beauty in it. And yes, you can have a good time during it too. (Hard to imagine, right? I know. But if you think about it, you should always try to see the positive side in any situation if you want to rise above it.)

I think the key to overcoming this period in life is not to overcome it, but—as I said before—to embrace it. It's a time of change. It's not always fun but it's your first true test of how you'll cope with life. The truth is that there will always be hard times in your life. So learn from your quarterlife crisis as much as you can. In many cases, it will help you become stronger and mold you into an even better person.

Changing Perspectives

So far, having a quarterlife crisis doesn't sound like too much fun now, does it? In many ways, it's not. But once you can shift your perspective, you may be able to benefit from, or even enjoy, this period of mass confusion. After all, you're in your 20s—you're not supposed to have it all figured out!

Melissa says that you have to look at a quarterlife crisis as exciting, instead of scary. "Most of us go from four or five years in college, living it up and partying on weekends and having a lot of free time, to then having to work 40+ hours per week, pay bills and manage our own finances. You see articles about 'save this much for retirement' and 'you should buy a house by this age' and it makes you start to wonder if you are moving too fast or too slow or behind the average person your age," she explains. Although college does have stress attached to it, Melissa feels that it is "relatively painless" compared to life after college. She says that students take courses during college to prepare them for a job, but these classes cannot prepare students for inner-office relationships, dealing with clients and vendors, true multi-tasking, plus the balance of home life and finances with your career.

"After graduating, you feel pressure to get the best job at some crazy high-paying amount (which rarely happens), live in a great apartment, and immediately settle down and think about marriage too," continues Melissa, who works as a marketing communications coordinator. She says most graduates also have to deal with debt from school loans that now have to be repaid and credit cards opened while on spring break freshman year, that have now racked up into the thousands. "You have to learn to balance paying those off, as well as paying current, new bills, and you have to watch out about getting into more debt now that you can afford (once you get a job, of course) to actually buy fun stuff for yourself every once in awhile and go out to dinner. It's hard to fine-tune that balance and it can take some many years to get to the point where they are financially savvy."

Not Your Parents' Experience

The concept of pressure rings true with so many facets of the quarter-life crisis. One problem Lacey sees is dealing with parents and family members. In her case, her parents did not attend college but got married young. She says they treat her as if any woman at 28 (her age at the time of publication) who has not married or had children is never going to achieve happiness. "It's just crazy! Most women I know are 28 to 30, single or in happy relationships, and still no home ownership or kids. And that is how they want it and may keep things for years to come," states Lacey. "But the parents and grandparents are pushing for marriage, kids and a home where they can come visit you and stay for days!" Props to her for having such a strong attitude; some graduates interpret that kind of pressure as one more thing they have to worry about.

Lacey is finding solace in friends to get her through her quarterlife crisis. Some of her family members have been understanding, but she notes that others still seem to think people are failures if they don't have it all by the mid- to late 20s. "Sometimes it does make you wonder if you are heading down the wrong path or that something is wrong with you. But friends in similar places as you can help make you realize that you really are a success if you are working hard, still trying to have fun on weekends, and are trying to be a good person in the world through volunteering and taking self-help classes, for example."

Lacey has a theory about adults who put pressure on their kids upon graduating. "Maybe it is the older generation wanting to live vicariously through us, hoping that we will somehow come out far better than they think they did, but in the end they are just putting undue pressure on us young adults who need to approach life our own way and on our own time schedule . . . and not theirs." While that's a good point, other grads know that their parents are just looking out for them.

The Early QLC

Melissa's interpretation of the quarterlife crisis is a little bit different than mine, but it still touches on the same main points. She believes crisis occurs after graduates get a job and then begin to panic about other facets of life. Other graduates believe the panic sets in upon graduation before they even get their first job. Two different viewpoints, but it all adds up to the same thing: quarterlife crisis.

Samantha says she experienced anxiety after college about what her next step or steps in life would be. She was worried about how she was going to pay rent, bills, student loans and take care of her car—mostly financial anxieties. Then came the pressure from her dad to be a "professional" even though she knew she wasn't a corporate ladder climber. With her degree in writing, Samantha thought she'd be the artsy type. That didn't pan out either. Instead, she has a good balance using her writing skills in a practical office work job that pays the bills and affords her the time to pursue creative endeavors on the side.

"I have a really good job and it took me a while to get here, but I did it without pushing and shoving my way into the job," explains Samantha. "I wouldn't say I put any pressures on myself after graduating other than to simply be able to afford the basics—rent, car expenses, food, clothes, a little bit of fun, etc." So what got her through her quarterlife crisis? Her family. Even now, in her mid 30s, she says she can still lean on them when she needs support.

Erika experienced worry about post-college life before she even put on her cap and gown. She graduated in December, when most of her friends were still in school and not slated to graduate until May. "I felt kind of alienated from them, because they were still taking classes and reading and writing papers and taking tests, and I was at home all day watching reruns on cable, knitting, and looking for a job. Graduating from college was an awful time for me."

Erika took a few months off deliberately to de-stress from her last semester, which she says was very intense. Until she found a job six months later, she was pretty miserable. "I was unemployed and idle for six months total. Six months is a long time to be bored, and boredom is the handmaiden of depression." Certainly worrying about all these issues before she graduated—and then feeling out of place for six months afterward—is enough to put anyone into crisis mode. She put a lot of weight on her first job as do many college graduates. When that doesn't turn into what you expected, you will be let down because you see that life outside of college is not what you had in mind. The emotions that go along with that are another aspect of the crisis.

While she did very well academically in college, Erika was worried about finding a good job that would pay her decent money and that she would enjoy. So on top of being alone, the job hunt itself was pretty stressful. She says she knew what she wanted to do, which was go to graduate school. Yet she also knew that she needed to take a year off. "What I didn't know was what I wanted to do in the working world—or what I even stood a chance of convincing some HR person that I was capable of doing. Or whether I'd be able to stand it once I had a job."

Erika summed up her first six months after graduating in this rant: "Is there anything more stressful than job hunting? It's the most incredibly stressful thing, because if you don't find a job, you starve, right? Starve or move back in with your parents, which no one wants to do. And even if you do get a job, and it pays enough, and you can be certain of affording to live on your own and not starve, you might still wind up finding a job that it turns out you hate. A job that you hate is a very special kind of hell, because if it's full time, that's at least 40 hours of every week consumed by hatred, and that takes a huge toll on a person."

I kept her full quote in complete context to show you the thoughts that many students and recent grads experience. It's a lot of back and forth—you need a degree to get a job, you don't know what you want to do, you want to do something meaningful—the list goes on. Luckily, Erika did find a job, which helped her feel better in many ways. "I felt materially better. My job paid rather a lot. I felt better because I knew that I was definitely employable. I felt better because I knew that I could survive outside of college, that I was capable of finding a great job and doing it well," she comments.

Even though Erika wanted to go back to school, taking that break and finally getting a job did help, even if it wasn't her ideal. And that's what I want to stress—you may want your ideal job right now. But if you can't get it, consider that sometimes it's good to just get out of the house and make some money so you don't go nuts locked inside. "There were a lot of jobs that I felt were beneath me as a college graduate. I didn't want to work retail. I didn't want to work food service. I didn't even want to do these things temporarily while looking for a real job," admits Erika, who subsequently did enter graduate school. Even though she managed to get a well-paying job, "There was a lot of boredom and depression and rejection on the way to it."

You do emerge. Life will get better if you happen to go through a quarterlife crisis. I'm just showing you what it entails so you don't think you're the only one experiencing what Erika and others have felt. *Most graduates go through a quarterlife crisis, and the feelings you'll go through while in it are very common.*

Now that the term quarterlife crisis is more widely recognized, it's opening up an array of resources and knowledgeable experts to help recent grads through tough times. If nothing else, it's validating the issues that you're probably dealing with already. I'm confident The After-College will get there too.

Lindsey Pollak is one person who understands the struggles that recent graduates face. She's the author of *Getting from College to Career: 90 Things to Do Before You Join the Real World*, a book she penned to give students practical advice before graduation day—and a subsequent quarterlife crisis—begins. Her book features practical, easy tips on finding a segue into professionalism. In it, she covers how to use thank-you notes, how to succeed in an internship—and even the 10 greatest American movies of all time that you should watch. Pollak's tips help make the dive into adulthood a little easier, perhaps preventing a quarterlife crisis.

Staying Social During Your QLC

One of the ways to cope with a quarterlife crisis is to rely on others for support. So if your best college buddy is across the miles, or even if you're looking for some new pals, Pollak offers the following tips for creating a new friendship—or even a few:

○ Join professional associations in your industry or any industry that you might want to work in someday, particularly "young professionals" groups within associations. This will help you make friends and make career networking connections.

○ Join an athletic team or club—softball, volleyball, basketball, running, anything. This is a great way to meet other young, active people. These teams are usually very social as well as helping you burn off calories and burn off steam. And you don't have to be that athletic. My younger sister moved to Japan for a teaching job after college and she made tons of friends there by joining the triathlon club—and she'd never done a triathlon in her life!

○ Join your college alumni association. If you live in an urban area, there is probably an alumni club of your university or perhaps your Greek organization. This is an easy way to connect with people who share an affinity. You can usually find such groups on Facebook.com.

If you follow the gist of Pollak's tips, it is to *join*. There are many social challenges that recent grads face after graduation. But the most important thing is to be constantly meeting new people to enlighten and support you as you grow. It takes initiative—so you'll have to get out there!

When Worry Turns into Panic

Here's something I can attest to: Life after graduation can make you ill. As someone who coped with anxiety (especially during my early 20s), I can tell you that the worst part of being in the midst of a quarterlife crisis is when it affects you physically. It's very common for recent grads to experience panic and depression, especially if they are genetically prone to it. It's probably an extreme, but it does happen. I wanted to shed light on this not only because I was personally affected by it, but because I know there are many more out there who face the same struggle.

Jessica, whom we met in Chapter 3, says she's experienced feelings of uncertainty concerning her decisions. She studied stage management, technical theater and design at Mountview Academy for Performing Arts in London and has since gone back to school for a law degree at the University of Glasgow in Scotland. She plans to study law and combine it with her background in media to work on the legal side of theater or television. Still, the somewhat drastic change in educational focus was enough for her to doubt herself, especially when she began to compare herself to others.

"At this age, we start to look at the other, younger people starting work around us and there's a feeling of envy there. These people still have all the choices ahead of them, whereas we're stuck with what we've done so far, and we start to look at our lives and wonder if we've done the right things," Jessica remarks. While the quarterlife crisis isn't solely about being envious of others younger than we are who don't have to face the decisions we do, this can bring on quarterlife crisis-related feelings.

Pursuing a higher degree has caused Jessica to doubt what she's doing. "I panic quite frequently now, more so than I did when I graduated the first time. Then, I had a job secured and I still felt like I had a load of time to do what I wanted. Now I'm a mature student in a degree course with people six or seven years my junior, and I do wonder if I'm too old to be still trying to cut out a career for myself," she confides. For a while, Jessica experienced many feelings of depression and worried that she would complete her graduate-level studies and not know what she wanted to do, or not be a prime job candidate. "I'm not so bad now," she notes. "I had a long talk with the chief advisor of studies at [my] university and have a better idea of my future options, but for a while I did have feelings of depression and worry."

Jessica also met a friend in Glasgow who worked for regional television broadcaster, Scottish Television. She got a part-time job there while she studies law. "I do feel much better now being back involved in the subject I originally trained for, as my adverse reaction to it really was more against my college than against the entertainment industry in general, and I feel now that I can say to my parents that they didn't waste their money."

Andrea states that she experienced a quarterlife crisis after earning her Master's degree, although it actually started after her undergraduate years at the University of Dallas. "I began breaking out in acne. This was very strange because I had never had skin problems before. I attribute this directly to my fear and anxiety about graduation," she says. After Andrea secured plans to go into graduate school, her anxiety ceased. She believes that her emotional state was due to the fact that there wasn't a program to prepare graduates for the working world. "I was told by one of my professors that I needed to get some 'marketable skills' after graduating," recalls Andrea. "This was disconcerting considering I had just spent $7,000 per semester." With a comment like that, who can blame her for freaking out a little? Andrea says her anxiety was situational, but it was certainly real. She remembers sleeping a lot. "I think the anxiety was manifested both physically and also mentally, but that is difficult to describe. I guess my mind was trying to sort itself out. [There were] so many things to choose from for a future, only one life, which path to take," she explains.

Carrie is certain that she experienced a quarterlife crisis. She says it happened when she questioned who she was and what she was doing. "My quarterlife crisis was very much about how I would distinguish myself from others in the world, what I would do different, and how I would be remembered," recalls Carrie, a graduate of Morehead State University and George Mason University. One thing that was added was anxiety. "I have a lot of anxiety," Carrie says. "We all strive to be successful—however it is we define that word—and it's overwhelming the lives we all live these days."

Still today, Carrie says that she experiences severe anxiety symptoms. "My anxiety occurs in the form of becoming fanatically overwhelmed and simply panicking. It's best described in regard to an unraveling blanket: you pull one thread and others unattach, creating other problems," she confides. About five years ago, Carrie was advised to take medication. "I was extremely hesitant. I was not one who believed in the power of pills, but rather the power of patience," recalls Carrie. At the time she was going through a divorce, however, and says her patience ran thin. She listened to her doctor and went on a prescription for six months. Carrie still takes her medication, and she says it does help. "Every six months for the past five years, he [my doctor] asks if I want to try going off the medication, and I always find some overwhelming life circumstance that shakes my head no," she reports. "I've tried going off the medication and find that my anxiety comes back with a vengeance; not so much a physical problem, as much as a panic, intense crying, heavy breathing, and general state of panic. Sleep is always better when I'm on the medication."

In Carrie's case, she's past her quarterlife crisis, but the anxiety that emerged during that time still exists. There could be a number of other reasons for it, but I wanted to illustrate that sometimes people face physical and mental issues as a result of the quarterlife crisis. As Carrie said, we live in a very stressful world, so it's common for people to experience anxiety after a time of crisis. I still get anxious from time to time and my quarterlife crisis is way behind me. But it was that time in my life when I was introduced to the anxiety monster.

Kelly understands anxiety. She says that although she is 27, she is still experiencing a quarterlife crisis. Unfortunately, hers has included panic attacks. "Thinking about life after college was pretty much one of the largest causes of this," says Kelly, who was featured in Chapter 2. But panic attacks are nothing new to her—Kelly has had anxiety issues since she was a child. She says she has put a lot of pressure on herself to succeed. "I want to make my parents proud. I want to be fulfilled and stable. This translates to all areas of my life—career, finances, relationships, etc.," adds Kelly. "I've put so much pressure on myself over these last few years that I believe it has contributed to my panic/anxiety disorder." Luckily, she is able to lean on her fiancé for support. Her family has been supportive too, but she says that she is not sure if they know how to help her. Some friends haven't been helpful, Kelly confides. "The older I have become, the more I have started to pull away. I don't want to burden anyone with my own quarterlife crisis," she says.

Most definitely, there is embarrassment associated with panic disorder, anxiety, and depression—or any mental issue, for that matter. Equally, coping with a quarterlife crisis can make people feel shameful. Just because you feel a little anxiety doesn't mean you have a mental disorder; the time after college is a huge transition that will naturally produce stress. As many grads turn to friends and family for support, they find that not everyone will help, or knows how to. If you're dealing with any life-interrupting emotional problems, it's important to get help from supportive friends, or even a professional. You don't have to live so uncomfortably, and gaining clarity during a tough time will better equip you for the future.

The Depressing Side of Things

Shannon, who graduated from University of Alberta in Canada, said she has experienced depression since she completed her undergraduate education. "After graduating I felt a sense of hopelessness, like there were no real opportunities out there with my degree. I had no idea what to do and was very, very concerned for my future," recalls Shannon, who graduated with a degree in physical education and had a hard time getting a job in her field. "Probably the most frustrating part of it all was that I didn't really know what I was passionate about in terms of a career. Therefore it made trying to find a job that I would enjoy remarkably hard. I'd get up in the morning and do job searches but nothing really seemed to 'turn me on.' This led to many feelings of worry and anxiety over how I would pay for bills in the coming future."

Shannon says that the greatest pressure put on her during this time was by her parents and herself. "I guess I always figured that upon graduating I would find a job in my field and that would be that. Little did I know that this is not at all how it works in the real world," she confides. Shannon adds that her parents pushed her to get a job and they expected her to "be set." Luckily, her friends were there to help her through the tough time and to offer sound advice. "I also turned to my faith in God to help me put things in perspective and [to help me] keep believing that everything would work out in the end."

Shannon was working as a freelance writer and headed back to school to pursue a career as a high school science teacher at the time of publication. She concludes that the quarterlife crisis is directly related to problems such as depression, alcohol, and drug abuse in young people today.

High Expectations, High Pressure

Kiki Weingarten, a career and education coach and co-founder of New York City-based www.dailylifeconsulting.com, agrees that pressure and high expectations can bring on quarterlife crisis. She knows that getting help—whether you're experiencing emotional or mental issues—

related to a quarterlife crisis is vital. Weingarten says the quarterlife crisis may be a result of the intense pressure that many students feel when trying to distinguish themselves early on. "Many of my clients are exhausted by the time they reach their first jobs. They've worked so hard in high school to get to the right college, in college to get into the right grad school, and in grad school to get the right job," she explains. "Then they look at their lives and say 'Is this what I want to do for the next 40 years?'"

Because school is so different from the working world, unprepared students can feel shocked when making the transition. Weingarten states that even students who are on track to get what they planned can feel confused. "This leads to feelings of depression and anxiety among a whole host of other issues," she adds. Weingarten relates that being independent for the first time, having financial responsibilities, facing educational debt, not having a built-in social system, and being low on the work totem pole can be scary for many students, producing anxiety and depression.

When students anticipate these issues and plan to face them, it can help. Weingarten recommends talking to those in your chosen career field, conferring with other graduates, and discussing things with a mentor or coach. This should help students feel better about facing their future and it can alleviate pangs associated with the quarterlife crisis. She notes that when she consults with clients, she teaches them to identify and develop skills they can use to adapt to situations during the crisis mode. Finding a strong center and sense of self—as well as a support system—is vital to help panicked individuals get through hard times. "Life is a series of changes and adventures. Learning how to deal with them constructively at a younger age gives students a head start to a successful future," Weingarten concludes.

Post-College Purgatory

Emily recalls having a "freak-out" after her last college exam at Boston University. "I wandered around the city of Boston for hours, not speaking to anyone, just knowing that if I stopped moving, I would break down. I felt totally inadequate and unprepared for any job, I had no job leads and no money, the lease on my apartment was nearly up, and I felt as though everyone else my age was at least somewhat better prepared than I was," she recalls. While she still feels that way, Emily says it's less intense. She has indeed struggled with aspects of the quarterlife crisis. She says she puts too much pressure on herself, but it's hard not to. "I have many talented friends who graduated from top schools and had companies fighting to hire them, and it's difficult to look to them and compare our post-graduate situations." Emily notes that even some of her older friends who have been out of school for a few years say they are still in the midst of a quarterlife crisis.

Emily's crisis revolves around her job—or lack thereof. At the time of publication, she did not yet have a salaried job but was using connections through her marketing internship to find a permanent gig. "The frustration of being in this kind of career limbo, watching the date my apartment lease is up looming ahead and having no ability to plan what to do or where to go until I can find a job is extremely difficult," she says. Fortunately, she's been able to rely on friends her age who are going through the same thing, but she says that it's "unpleasant" to try and discuss it with anyone else.

"I think a big part of anxiety over a quarterlife crisis is that it's not recognized the same way a midlife crisis would be. A midlife crisis is something that a person has, so to speak, *earned* by being 'weighed down' by family, jobs and aging. A quarterlife crisis is theoretically not so bad because its sufferers are young and supposedly have the world at their fingertips," Emily explains. "It's hard to get someone to take your concerns seriously when you're only 21."

What's most frustrating for Emily is hearing people who have pushed through "post-graduate purgatory" tell her not worry about life. "It's nauseating to hear, because I don't care about the rest of my life at the moment. I care that my rent gets paid next month. I care that I have a job at the end of the summer. I care about now," she says. I absolutely understand her frustration. On top of going through a quarterlife crisis, it can be infuriating when someone blows it off. Going through a quarterlife crisis is horrible. It is frustrating. And it is scary!

CHAPTER 11

Ramen Noodles, Rent, Resumes . . . and Real Life

"Livin' it up!"

When I set out to write this book, I wanted to write about a topic I knew well. Having almost survived my 20s—and one nasty quarterlife crisis—I felt that there was a need to provide some guidance for students who had just graduated from college or graduate school. But more importantly, I wanted it to be okay for students struggling to see that others were doing the same. College is commonly viewed as preparation for the real world, but I knew that it was normal for people to realize that attending four years of school *didn't* equip them for the challenges they would face—and that was okay. I'm a big believer in the power of anecdotes and real-life experiences to comfort and motivate us, so I chose to interview students about the various topics featured in the book. I hope their honesty, coupled with the revelations that it's okay to feel how you feel, help you along your way. Knowing this, I'm confident that you can make it through whatever your 20s throw at you.

When I left Stockton on May Day, I didn't know anything about a quarterlife crisis. Had I, I would have probably dreaded life after college even more. Once I got out of school, life wasn't too great for me. But now that I've found my soul's work, discovered who my real friends are, learned how to be financially savvy, figured out how to clean a dryer vent and write a killer resume, I want people to know that life after college need not be dreaded. While scary, it doesn't have to be a total wash out. Yes, it's easier for me to say that because I've been through it all, but I also believe that with a little insight and a lot of perspective, you can thrive in The After-College. Note how I didn't say that you could avoid the stumbles I made? I wouldn't want you to not experience hardships and heartbreak—those are the things that help you grow. Those are the things that shape you into an even better you. An adult you.

Who will you be? Think about it, yes. But don't feel like you've got to have it all figured out. Just for now, just for your After-College, experience life without too many things holding you down. Travel, spend time with friends, take that cool job you've always wanted . . . because you *can*.

Throughout most of my After-College, I thought it all was a quarterlife crisis. I was overwhelmed by the challenges most of the time. When you emerge from something, you're always wiser, and I hope my wisdom will help you. Life in your 20s doesn't have to be a crisis. The period of time known as The After-College can have just as much joy as hardship. You have to inject the joy because the challenges can get overwhelming. But once you do, you'll realize how cool this time in your life is. (Even if you're unlike me and were looking forward to it on the day you graduated!)

Looking Ahead

Richard Marquis, who was featured in Chapter 2, makes a good point about living in your 20s. "College is about immersing yourself in your studies, learning everything you can, and grabbing the grades you need to succeed. *Life* is about reinterpreting these skills within the context of new goals, applications and rewards," he states.

Lindsey Pollack, an author featured in Chapter 6, says that college is a great time to explore and expand your horizons, so it's okay not to feel entirely prepared to enter the real world. Doesn't that make you want to sigh with relief? You don't have to have it all together. That's the real essence of The After-College. It's in the not knowing what lies ahead, but looking bravely ahead to the future. Along the way, it's okay to look back. But *do* keep looking forward.

Nearly a year before this book was published, my husband and I bought our first house. We had been married for two years and lived in the same apartment for nearly five. It was time to do the adult thing and settle down. These things would have been monumentally scary for me thinking about them at 22. But in going through The After-College, I realized that they weren't. I had evolved into an adult. It wasn't so scary like I thought it would be.

It was cool to finally have my own home. After so many years of wonder and doubt, there I was all alone in my new office. Boxes and crates were scattered around the room and my precious Dell was plugged in. It was the only thing functioning in the room. Me and my laptop. Me and this book.

I yanked out a cardboard box full of everything that was on my desk in our old apartment. Should I hang a picture of my beloved grandmother or my cat? Both passed on during my 20s, making it almost unbearable at times. Or should I hang up a positive quote? Maybe I should put up that picture of Heather, my friend from high school who has seen me through it all. I pulled out a postcard. It was one of those enlarged ones, half the size of a normal piece of paper. On it was an aerial view of Stockton's campus lake, which was surrounded by pine trees I knew all too well. In small letters in the corner was the return address: The Stockton College Alumni Association. In big letters across the center were the words "Come Home."

Seven years ago, I would have given everything to go back to my school in the woods: To go back to the only place that ever really felt like home to me. To go back to the place where I had the times of my life. To go back to the place where I was untroubled, not worrying about a job or an apartment or money.

But not this day. On this particular day, I thought about how I was thrust into The After-College. I kicked and screamed most of the way, but eventually, I did find my way. I may have been carefree in college, but I had no idea what life was really like as an adult. Now that I'm out here living it, I have to tell you, it's pretty darn good.

Appendices

Appendix A
Cool Post-College Resources

www.twentyhood.com: A podcast about 20-something life

www.nomoreramenonline.com: Job search tools, video diaries and more

www.pursuethepassion.com: A project in determining career satisfaction

www.quarterlifecrisis.com: Message boards and other 20-something resources

www.roadtripnation.com: Site about e-road trips

www.hatchmagazine.com: A magazine focusing on 20-somethings

www.elearners.com: Directory for online learning opportunities

www.apartments.com: Find a place to call your own

www.helpmeharlan.com: A cool dude answers all your college questions

www.boomerangnation.com: Site devoted to moving back in with your parents

www.lifeaftercollegeproject.com: A project dedicated to the psychology of life after college

www.gradspot.com: A site devoted to life after college

www.doesyourmajormatter.com: Blog from Katie Konrath about careers

Appendix B
Job Resources

www.monster.com: Job search database

www.craigslist.com: Job listings—and much more—in your area

www.careerbuilder.com: Top job hunting website

www.hotjobs.com: Yahoo's job board

www.salary.com: Find out how much you're worth

www.mediabistro.com: Great jobs in the media industry

www.freelanceswitch.com: Job boards and great advice for going self-employed

www.indeed.com: Searches multiple sites for a great listing of jobs in all industries

Appendix C
Financial Resources

www.debtadvice.org : The National Foundation for Credit Counseling

www.debthelp.com: Offers debt management solutions

www.greenpath.com: Nonprofit organization offering free counseling

www.asec.org: The American Savings Education Council

www.bankrate.com: Features consumer loan rates

www.practicalmoneyskills.com: Offers practical financial management skills

www.allstudentloan.com: Financial tools and consolidation services from nonprofit lenders

www.youngmoney.com: Start saving and investing—helpful tools free here

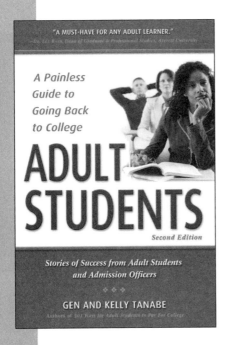

GET MORE TOOLS AND RESOURCES FOR GRADUATE SCHOOL AT SUPERCOLLEGE.COM

Visit www.supercollege.com for more free resources on graduate school admission, scholarships, and financial aid, and apply for the SuperCollege Scholarship, which is open to graduate students.

K risten Fischer is a copywriter and author living at the Jersey Shore. Her first book, *Creatively Self-Employed: How Writers and Artists Deal with Career Ups and Downs* was released in 2007.

She received her Bachelor's degree in environmental studies from The Richard Stockton College of New Jersey in 2000. Kristen attributes much of her happiness during college to being a member of the community service organization Circle K International.

Upon graduation, Kristen worked as a newspaper reporter and technical writer. In 2003, she launched her copywriting business and began writing books.

Kristen lives with her husband, Tim, and her cat, Bobbie. She enjoys spending time with family and friends, reading, knitting, kayaking, and frequenting Starbucks.

For more about her, visit www.kristenfischer.com.